The UK Cohousing Network

Practical Guide to Cohousing

For Cohousing Communities, Community Led Housing Hubs and Stakeholder Organisations

funded by

The final editors of this revised Guide have been Martin Field, Jonathan How and Chris Coates.

The information for the whole work was produced by a team co-ordinated by East Midlands Community Led Housing that included Martin Field, Chris Coates, Bob Colenutt, Dan Fitzpatrick, Iqbal Hamiduddin, Jonathan How, Jim Hudson, Georgia Laganakou, Trish McCourt and Debbie Seaborn.

Supplementary material has been provided from a UKCN 'Diversity and Inclusion sub-group' that included Yael Arbell, Cynthia Brathwaite, Des Figuerido, David Francis, Bill Phelps, Maurice Woodbridge, Tim Woodward, and Claude Hendrickson, and other updates from Cohousing Scotland, contacts in Wales and in Northern Ireland.

Sincere thanks are extended to all the Cohousing groups, CLH Hubs and individuals who submitted comments and suggestions for this Guide.

Typesetting. design and layout by Coherent Visions.

First published in this format 2022 by
Diggers & Dreamers Publications, BCM Edge, London WC1N 3XX

ISBN-13: 978-1-838472528

Community Led Homes is a national partnership between the UK Cohousing Network, the Confederation of Co-operative Housing, the National Network of Community Land Trusts and Locality that is actively working to make it easier for communities to undertake all kinds of community-led housing initiatives.

Funded by

www.communityledhomes.org.uk

www.emclh.co.uk

"Cohousing communities are intentional communities, created and run by their residents. Each household has a self-contained, private home as well as shared community space. Residents come together to manage their community, share activities, and regularly eat together".

Foreword by UK Cohousing Network

We are delighted to welcome you to the UK's new comprehensive guide to Cohousing. Whether you are an adviser, a group, a council planner, developer or investor, or simply exploring the topic, this guide will provide you with all the foundations you need when considering cohousing.

This Guide arrives at a critical moment. The COVID-19 pandemic has raised significant questions for many of us about the way we live and whether our current housing system is fit for purpose with many left isolated or alone, many in poor housing.

Cohousing shows us that it doesn't need to be that way. Individual citizens and communities up and down the country are realising that they can find ways to design their own housing and create the neighbourhoods they want to live in; supportive, friendly and designed to be sustainable.

The current housing system works to make it feel very hard to develop alternatives to the limited choices on offer. However it can be done and in time will become easier. This is a guide to accompany you on your journey, drawn from the generously shared experiences of those bold pioneers who have gone before you. In drawing upon their lessons and advice, we hope the path of cohousing entrepreneurs of the future will be smoother and quicker.

Each project and community is unique and so you'll need to adapt these lessons to your own situation. Whatever your direction, there is no need to be alone - by joining the UK Cohousing Network you'll be able to connect with people and projects across the country and build a movement for future generations.

Angela Vincent and Owen Jarvis, UKCN

Here are some words of encouragement from members of the UK Cohousing Network's Board:

> *Best way I have ever lived! Cohousing creates a sort of modern tribe; a way that feels natural, like "coming home". There is a sense of well-being and security, of laughter with others and safety when things get difficult*
> *[Jackie Carpenter, Friendship Cohousing, Cornwall]*

> *Even if you vaguely like the sound of Cohousing, then it's almost certainly right for you. You might hear that it isn't easy - but how 'easy' are the other ways to find a home? Now that I've done it, I can't imagine living in any other way and there's so much more in the way of advice than there was 10 years ago when we started*
> *[Simon Bayly, Copper Lane Cohousing, London]*

> *It was great to be involved with the whole journey of design and development. It means you move in with a real sense of ownership beyond your front door and you have already got to know many of your neighbours. The sense of community on move in was instant.*
> *[Frances Wright, Marmalade Lane Cohousing, Cambridgeshire]*

www.cohousing.org.uk

How to use this Guide

Introduction

This Guide is an up-to-date summary of how to create new Cohousing projects in the UK, primarily in England.

It was funded by the UK Cohousing Network from the national Community Led Homes alliance and produced by a team of practitioners, researchers, designers and community activists co-ordinated by East Midlands Community Led Housing (one of the regional CLH-Hubs).

Its material has been collected from background research of relevant literature, reports and websites and from surveys, interviews and discussions with groups, members of the community-led housing sector and other stakeholders.

Focus of the Guide

This Guide is aimed mainly at groups and individuals who want to undertake a Cohousing project in which they will live themselves, to help the project be as strong and as dynamic as possible and to build clarity and confidence in the various tasks and steps that will turn initial ambitions into neighbourhood reality.

It starts from the assumption that the group or collection of households is committed to creating a new Cohousing project. It does not give consideration to everything that could be 'community-led' for people to then agree they want to develop a new Cohousing project; it assumes that people have already looked at those potential options and have already decided to build a project based on Cohousing's values.

[For further information on the broader community led housing sector please see the Resources section at the end of this publication]

The information in this Guide is divided into five elements:

- An abridged Guide

- The main Guide, which covers the key phases of Cohousing project development: Group, site, plan, build and live

- A section on Cohousing design principles

- Information about financial considerations and potential sources of funding

- Case studies and resources

Reference to the experience and results of other Cohousing projects has been included wherever feasible. Using tips and practices from other Cohousing projects can be very fruitful; there is no need for every new project to be entirely innovative in everything.

New Ground, North London

Layout of the Guide

The Guide is arranged in sections that projects will need to consider, moving from very initial scheme conceptions, through to final realisations and to occupation. It has adapted the project pipeline tasks used by CLH-Hubs:

- the initial stages in forming a group and setting a vision;

- finding a site or property to use;

- obtaining all the planning permissions and finances;

- undertaking the construction or renovation works;

- finally moving in and living as a new neighbourhood.

Look for these symbols

 A key design principle

 A key financial point

 Local authorities may consider developing a policy on this point

Information is laid out in double-page spreads. The LEFT hand side of each spread is focused on technical prompts and information that should be considered as a project moves through the sequential steps of bringing a property development project to fruition.

The PDF version of this Guide is interactive and includes links to relevant sections within it. The main section headings are shown on tabs on the right of each page. By clicking on any of the tabs readers can jump to that section of the document. Similar links are included throughout the Guide so that readers can navigate easily between sections. The "Questions asked about Cohousing" also provide direct links to a relevant double-page spread where information can be found on each question posed. [The PDF-version is not able to take the reader immediately back to a page they had just 'jumped away' from, but a click on one of the coloured tabs will connect to the contents of each section, and it should be easier to then move to the page previously being read.]

External hyperlinks (to useful reports, checklists, practitioner feedback, commentaries, etc) are also provided.

Each topic is presented on a two-page spread to enable groups to focus on discrete issues at their own pace. A small amount of information is duplicated by intention.

The Guide signposts readers to an abundance of advice and information from other sources. Groups should make sure this is properly considered.

The RIGHT hand side of each spread gives specific examples of relevant points that groups can consider.

Cohousing activists need to maintain a firm engagement with all elements of their project. The group's overall activities will take place throughout the lifetime of their scheme and will be more than the matters described in the Group stage.

Build

Live

Design

Finance

Questions asked about Cohousing

Page numbers given for print version but in the PDF version questions are clickable

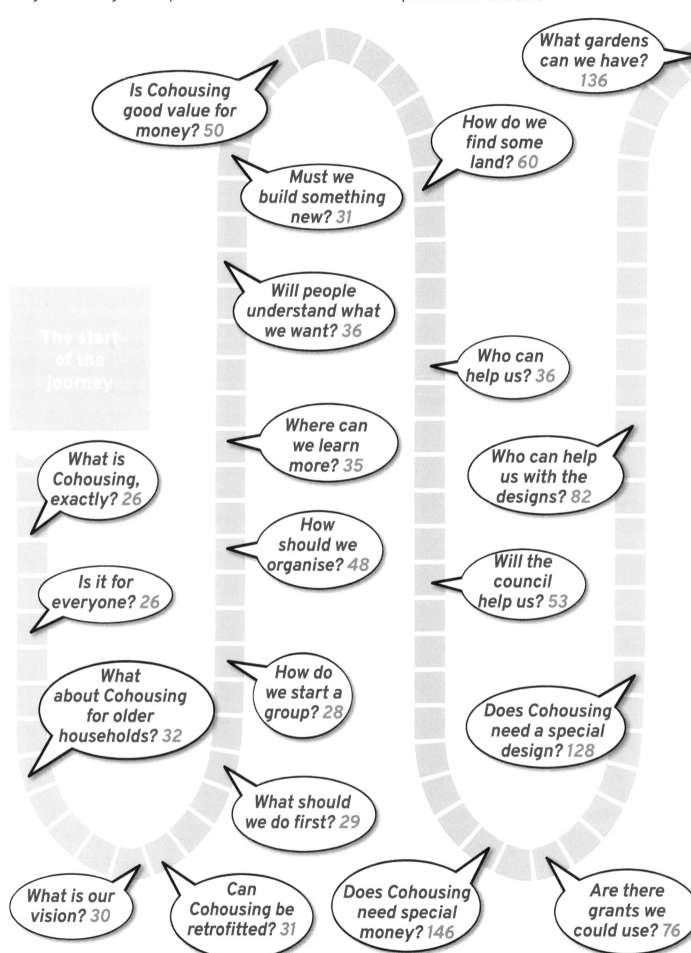

What gardens can we have? 136

Is Cohousing good value for money? 50

How do we find some land? 60

Must we build something new? 31

Will people understand what we want? 36

Who can help us? 36

The start of the journey

Where can we learn more? 35

Who can help us with the designs? 82

What is Cohousing, exactly? 26

How should we organise? 48

Is it for everyone? 26

Will the council help us? 53

What about Cohousing for older households? 32

How do we start a group? 28

Does Cohousing need a special design? 128

What should we do first? 29

What is our vision? 30

Can Cohousing be retrofitted? 31

Does Cohousing need special money? 146

Are there grants we could use? 76

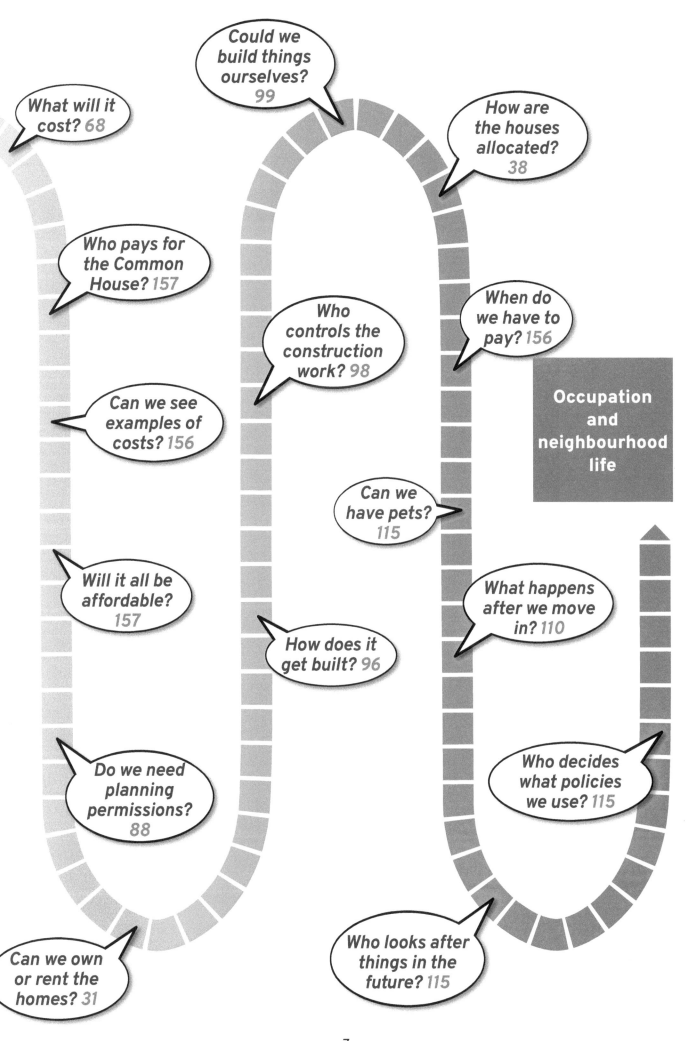

Springhill Cohousing, Stroud

Introduction

Key decisions for Cohousing projects

Cohousing is a model for neighbourhood initiatives that is a challenge to conventional housing development. Before starting a Cohousing development project, groups need to consider a number of aspects:

The basics

- Who is it for? Are the proposals for an intergenerational development, for a 'Senior' project for older households, or for a specific 'community of interest'?

- How big will it be? The optimum occupancy for a Cohousing development is between 20 and 50 adults.

- Will this be a new-build project, or a 'retrofit' one, remodelling existing buildings?

- Will it be for single tenure (all homeowners for example), a mix of tenures (ownership or rental tenures for the individual households), or a 'Mutual Home Ownership' scheme, in which a collectively-managed organisation owns the properties?

- What environmental standard is wanted from the final buildings? Note that this can impact on living costs when households take up occupation

Design

- How will the dwellings and other shared facilities be arranged on the site?

- How central will the Common House be?

- What will its intended function at the 'heart' of the neighbourhood be?

- What details will be incorporated to maximise contact between neighbours?

- How will the 'basic principles of Cohousing design' be used? (See the DESIGN section of this Guide)

Finances

- What potential sources of private and public finance will be available during the pre-development, planning approval and capital construction periods?

- How will you ensure sufficient cash flow is available to meet costs at each stage?

- What will the payments and service charges for Cohousing members be?

> **When I am asked whether Cohousing lived up to my expectations – my answer is: NO – My imagination wasn't this good. It far exceeds what I thought we would be able to achieve**
> **[Established community]**

Initial ideas for a Cohousing project

The founding momentum behind a new project could start from a collection of individuals sharing ideas, or from a local supporter with a potential site to use.

Group dynamics and decision-making

Having a plan and timetable to shape first activities is an opportunity for a group to practise working together before living together, minimising potential conflict.

Agreeing a vision and dealing with disagreements

A group should agree a vision for the project which reflects the key ideas, ethics and practical outcomes it wants to promote.

Support from CLH Hubs and Facilitators

Local community-led housing Hubs and Facilitators can help with many aspects of developing a Cohousing project including advocacy and support for community-building and property development.

Membership, diversity and inclusion

Groups need to find ways to include households from a potentially wide range of backgrounds at all stages in the project's development.

Legal incorporation

Groups will find it easier to move forward practically if they adopt a legal format used by other projects in similar circumstances; there is no need to spend time considering their long-term identity.

The social value of Cohousing

Cohousing can clearly demonstrate the social value that comes from projects designed to create dynamic and supportive neighbourhoods.

Finding external support

Projects seeking 'enabling' support from external partners should use a formal Memorandum of Understanding or Heads of Terms agreement as a basis for what such a partnership will entail.

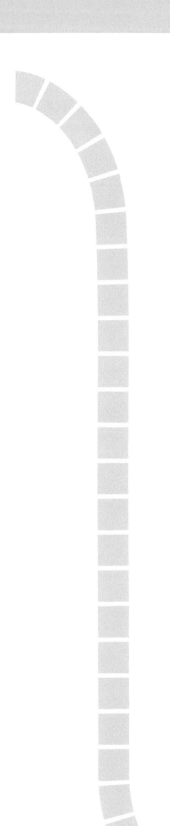

Making a search for land or property

Groups must be prepared to be proactive in order to make contact with land or property-owners.

Identifying land or property

Not all sites will be able to offer everything that a group might want it to. Be prepared to compromise on what is available; an indeterminate wait can become damaging to the group's existence.

Initial concepts – technical and social

The social and interactive success at the heart of Cohousing places is not arrived at accidentally – it is a combination of clear intent and astute design.

Considering a project manager role

A dedicated project manager could facilitate and inform the development of external partnerships. They could become an invaluable advocate on the project's behalf.

Feasibility studies and financial modelling

The finances involved in creating an holistic Cohousing setting need to be considered as a whole; there is no separation between the costs of constructing private spaces and communal spaces.

Heads of Terms for site acquisitions

Groups need to plan for schemes that can create the interpersonal dynamics evident in Cohousing areas elsewhere. On a new site this could mean between one and two acres, depending on the number of members and the group's intentions.

Producing a project business plan

Those evaluating a Cohousing business plan will ask:

● does its summary of the group's AMBITION give enough information for the reader who will not wade through every page?

● does the FLOW of the text give sufficient detail of how the Cohousing objectives and outputs will be achieved?

● do the FINANCIAL FORECASTS show that the Cohousing promoters can cope with changing circumstances?

Seeking funding for site and plan costs

Funding could already be needed at this stage for site acquisition and design works.

Selecting partners – if desired

It is crucial that a group's partners understand its Cohousing values through all the project's phases – from its inception through to completion and occupation.

Confirming architects, designers and other professionals

All appointed agents need to understand the project's values in all its phases – the Cohousers should have an input into how all appointments are made.

Final design – technical, social, communal

How much of the proposed final design has already been discussed with planners or with elected Councillors from the local authority? Has any of the design received negative responses to date?

Planning permissions and agreements

Groups should be aware that local requirements could require a Cohousing project to meet policy levels for economic affordability and inclusivity

Agreeing capital costs

All capital costs should be completed and agreed at this stage, ready to finalise the budget for construction.

Construction options

Groups need to understand that the construction stage is a crucial point at which external partners' potential costs and returns become most apparent.

Securing development finance

All finance for construction works needs to be secured before committing to a contract to start on-site works.

Appointing contractors

Groups must rigorously oversee the way that tendering and appointments are managed and should make sure they are integral to the formal appointment process, even if this is being co-ordinated by an external partner.

Agreeing the construction programme

Avoid allowing individual group members to tweak works to 'their property' once construction has started. Changes at this stage can delay the work and creates potential for disputes when final costs are apportioned to the group and to properties.

Homes under construction or renovation

Dealing with matters that come to light through the 'snagging' period can feel like it never has an end. Don't worry if this continues after people have moved in, as this is the time when members need to test the integrity of the buildings that have been delivered.

Live stage

Finalising sales, rents and service charges

All purchase and rental arrangements need to be finalised with each household before they move in.

Moving in

A number of things can be done as a community to make the move-in go as smoothly as possible and to support each other in what can be a stressful time.

Common meals

Cohousing communities generally share between two and five meals per week in their Common House. Eating common meals needs to be voluntary and numbers attending will vary from meal to meal.

Neighbourhood policies

Some Cohousing groups have a daunting list of policies, but there are some simple ground rules and tips. Groups do not need a full list of policies right away, but some things do need to be in place from the beginning.

Living in Cohousing

Remember the importance of people in all of this. Having meetings, getting agreements in place and deciding policies are essential, but bureaucracy should only further the aims of the group. If it doesn't work, it can be thrown out.

Cohousing home truths

Cohousing can be hard work and sometimes the going gets tough. if people want to live better lives in community together, then things must sometimes be done differently.

Sustaining the community's vision

It's worth now and then doing a reality check. As an individual, or as a group, ask: Did what was done live up to what was intended? Does it still pretty much work – as a community and for individual households?

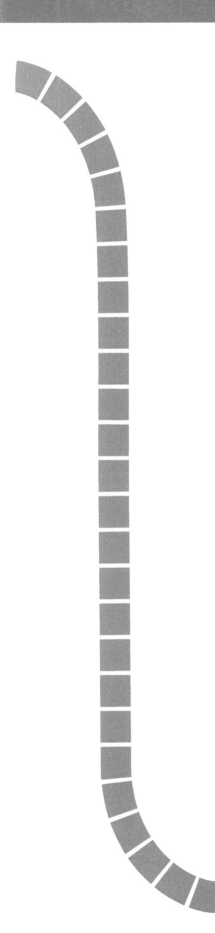

Key phases of project development

The Guide contains advice and information on a series of tasks and issues summarised under the main phases below. There is a usual sequence to these main phases and activities, and some of the issues within phases also follow on in a natural sequence. At times, actions will need to be undertaken simultaneously on more than one task. This is explained in the text.

Group	Site	Plan
A project's starting stage, building up initial membership, its legal status and its vision to live in shared neighbourhood	Seeking a suitable site (or existing property to remodel) for Cohousing, and some initial partners to support this vision	The formal design, approvals and costings for an identified site and confirmation of other partnerships, as required

Group

- Initial ideas for a Cohousing project
- Group dynamics and decision-making
- Agreeing the project's vision
- Dealing with disagreements and conflict
- Support from CLH-Hubs and Facilitators
- Membership and external communication
- Diversity and inclusion
- Legal incorporations
- The Social Value of Cohousing
- Finding external support

Site

- Making a search for land or property
- Identifying land or property
- Initial concepts – technical and social
- Considering a project manager role
- Feasibility studies and financial modelling
- Heads of Terms for site acquisitions

Plan

- Producing a project business plan
- Seeking funding for site and plan costs
- Selecting partners – if desired
- Confirming architects and designers
- Appointing other professionals
- Final design – technical, social, communal
- Approvals, regulations and agreements
- Agreeing capital costs

The main sections of the Guide (accessed by the tabs on the side) provide key advice and information relevant to each of these phases and signpost to other resources. There are also sections providing detailed information on Cohousing designs and Cohousing finances, along with useful links. The sections have been separated into sub-sections that align with the 'project pipeline' tasks already in use by Community Led Homes, which current CLH Facilitators and CLH-Hubs are already familiar with.

Build

The construction and completion stage, with on-site contractors being appointed and managed by a group or its agents

- Construction options
- Securing development finance
- Appointing contractors
- Agreeing the construction programme
- Homes under construction or renovation

Live

Building work is completed, properties are occupied, and the new community is embarking upon life within a shared neighbourhood

- Finalising sales, rents and service charges
- Moving in
- Common meals
- Neighbourhood policies
- Living in Cohousing
- Cohousing home truths
- Sustaining the community's vision

Design

- Basic principles of Cohousing site designs and layouts

Finance

- A summary of the funding required at each stage of project development

Resources

- The challenge to Cohousing and to Cohousing groups
- Schemes to compare with Cohousing
- Diversity and inclusion – challenging assumptions and overcoming barriers
- UK Cohousing examples
- Cohousing tenures
- Resources

The key characteristics of Cohousing projects

For this to be a useful guide to creating Cohousing projects and neighbourhoods in the UK, it will help to be clear on what is meant by the term 'Cohousing'. Not every collaborative or community-based housing scheme will be a 'Cohousing' one.

For the purposes of this Guide, 'Cohousing' projects are projects which have:

- decisions taken under the control of the prospective residents; it is the group that manages and is responsible for overseeing the co-design, co-development and co-organisation of the shared neighbourhood;

- a design of the physical form and layout of the neighbourhoods to maximise incidental and organised contact between residents;

- self-contained accommodation plus significant common facilities and spaces, of which a 'Common House' is a crucial setting for communal activities; common facilities operate as shared extensions to the dwellings and their amenities;

- an appropriate size and scale of each neighbourhood setting to underpin the sustainable community dynamics in that neighbourhood and for meaningful relationships to develop between its households.

Taken together, these features will sufficiently distinguish Cohousing projects from other collaborative housing or neighbourhood initiatives.

The fundamental basis underlying such Cohousing projects is the shared aspirations of its members to live as a group of neighbourly households, and a deliberate use of the best tools to realise those aspirations in the most dynamic and sustainable ways.

Threshold Centre, Dorset

Ambitions of Cohousing projects

The key principles noted here have informed a number of different kinds of Cohousing projects:

- intergenerational projects for a mix of ages and family-sized households (like Laughton Lodge, Forgebank, or Springhill);

- 'Senior' Cohousing projects, for households above a minimum age (usually aged 50+, such as Cannock Mill in England and the former Vivarium Trust and Pennington projects in Scotland);

- projects for just one gender (such as New Ground);

- projects for households with a distinct shared interest such as schemes based upon sexual orientation or looking at sharing additional responsibilities such as 'co-caring' responsibilities for vulnerable family members;

- projects for new-build properties (like Springhill) and projects that wish to 'retrofit' the character of Cohousing into an existing place – either in rural places like the Threshold Centre, or in urban settings like On the Brink or the Rainbow Housing Co-op.

Groups might attach to their Cohousing ambitions certain ideas that projects need to have a particular identity – such as being a 'co-op' or being 'ecological'. However, there is no single legal structure that must be used as a formal basis for a Cohousing project.

Groups who wish to end up with particular built and shared outcomes may need to consider certain legal structures, so comment has been provided in the GROUP section for groups to look at options for their own formal identities.

The FINANCE section gives information about how to deal with the variety of costs that Cohousing projects entail. There is no minimum requirement for a Cohousing project to provide a pre-determined number of residences with a particular tenure or mix of tenures. The types of tenure are, however, likely to be of crucial importance to the members of the project, and will probably be a key factor in any household remaining a member of the group.

Groups will also need to prepare for educating potential supporters and local stakeholders about their intentions to develop dynamic neighbourhood relationships. Not all external perceptions of Cohousing will necessarily be in line with their own.

An informative visual introduction to such collaborative housing projects can be found at this link:

www.vimeo.com/170652492

Cohousing:
The myths and the realities

The following explains some of the wider socio-political context in which Cohousing can be viewed in the UK.

Myths	Realities
Cohousing is demanding, time-consuming and too difficult to be an option for many.	There is an abundant appetite at community level for new schemes, but this cuts across the standard UK practice of housing being provided for others (mainly individuals) to buy or rent. It is evident that there is a persistent uncertainty within regulatory and other housing bodies about how to respond to group-led initiatives, which has led to long delays in previous efforts to bring projects together.
Cohousing is unaffordable for many and has no wider benefit – it promotes self-selection and gated communities.	The Cohousing vision to create vibrant and supportive neighbourhoods is one that is open to All. The means to make that a reality in the UK have at times been difficult to achieve when the UK land and housing markets have been so expensive. Cohousing groups have routinely started with a wide range of initial members but have often not found the support from external stakeholders to put an inclusive vision into practice.
The principles of Cohousing can be found in a variety of small and large schemes, depending on what local people want: a Common House and other shared facilities are not essential parts of all Cohousing schemes.	There are many kinds of collaborative housing projects. Misunderstanding can still be found about what underpins 'Cohousing' dynamics. Projects wanting to replicate the key dynamics of successful schemes accept that a Common House will be at the heart of the neighbourhood.
Cohousing is not a form of 'community led housing' as it does not need to provide affordable units	Cohousing has a neighbourhood focus to its values and is a model completely accountable to its community members and their resources. Projects have provided properties for sale, rent and shared ownership.
It is more difficult to find a site for Cohousing than for other community-led housing models.	Cohousing schemes tend to be larger than other community initiatives. This means that Cohousing groups are more likely to be in direct competition withother housebuilders for suitable sites.

Myths	Realities
Developer-led schemes are the key route to future success.	Benefit will be gained from some developer-enabled schemes, but groups need to lead on the costs and outcomes involved in creating such partnerships..
There should not be any subsidising of Cohousing for sale or for private ownership.	UK Cohousing schemes have had minimal public funds to date. If future schemes are to meet mixed-tenure housing policies, then private funds will cover most tenures; public funds might help in providing some tenures.
The shared facilities in a Cohousing scheme are a luxury that may not be affordable.	There may be upfront costs in providing shared facilities for a Cohousing scheme (e.g. Common House, laundry, car club etc) but the long-term savings for individual households can be enormous. From the wider perspective of reducing consumption, a Cohousing scheme can be an excellent exemplar to its surrounding community – proving that it is possible to live a very acceptable lifestyle while dramatically reducing carbon emissions.
A lot of projects go 'wrong' and there is not enough said or written about that.	Can Cohousing projects go wrong? Yes, of course. Groups can disband when they fail to find the kind of site they are looking for or members fail to agree on how they might proceed cohesively. A completed scheme could also fail to create the harmonious neighbourhood dynamic that its members have wanted.
	Projects can also be financially mismanaged or end up too expensive. Property development is, in itself, very challenging and Cohousing groups will face all the same challenges plus others that might arise when people are working and living closely together.
	A major aim of this Guide is to steer people away from some of the snares that can bring groups and their projects to a dead-end.

Build

Live

Finance Design

Across the UK...

This Cohousing Guide was financed through the Community Housing Fund, established by the Westminster government primarily to support community-led projects across England. By necessity, and by the nature of the examples quoted, more information is contained that details projects in England than in the other regions.

Housing and planning legislation in both Scotland and Wales are 'devolved' responsibilities, meaning the national governments and assemblies have responsibility for determining what housing ideals are set and what resources are directed towards them. Some introductory information is set out here on initiatives and work that is under way in Scotland, Wales and Northern Ireland, and it is hoped that future editions of the Guide can contain further practical uses of the legal and financial frameworks that exist in the different parts of the UK.

Much of the general advice provided here is, however, focused on how projects can be set up, and how groups can agree their visions and their aims for the future and progress with meaningful partnerships and professional support. This advice should thereafter be as helpful to groups across the UK as drawn from their counterparts in England.

Scotland

The situation around Cohousing in Scotland is different in a number of ways to that in the rest of the UK. Crucially, Scotland has its own legal system, property law, planning system and support for social / affordable housing. Scotland has a distinct approach to land ownership and is investigating land reform.

Scotland is home to a variety of longstanding intentional communities including Laurieston Hall, several Camphill Communities and Findhorn Ecovillage - with two contrasting Cohousing projects - Soillse and East Whins.

For many years there have been groups active in Scotland working to establish Cohousing projects, including Vivarium Trust in Fife, Penington Senior Cohousing and Clachan Cohousing in Glasgow, CHOISS - Cohousing in Southern Scotland, Hope Cohousing in Orkney and others.

Vivarium Trust was established in 2007 as a charity with a focus on Cohousing for older people and commissioned Arc Architects to publish 'Cohousing - future homes for older Scots' in 2018. The group's recommendations to a Scottish Government Working Group in 2019 included the need for a series of pilot projects to develop a template that could be followed by communities across Scotland. The Scottish Government published a new Housing Strategy: Housing to 2040 in 2021. Cooperative housing and Cohousing both receive favourable mention as delivery models which 'would be beneficial.'

Since 2021 Cohousing Scotland (www.cohousing.scot) acts as a support forum for local groups, fostering best practice, promoting opportunities and providing guidance to stakeholders. It lobbies decision-makers, advises on policy and promotes all the benefits of Cohousing. The organisation hosts online Cohousing Conversations and publishes a regular eNewsletter. In 2021 Cohousing Scotland published a manifesto for all forms of community Led and Co-operative Housing (CLaCH) providers.

The Communities Housing Trust, South of Scotland Community Housing and Rural Housing Scotland facilitate community-led housing projects.

Northern Ireland

A new housing supply strategy is being developed for Northern Ireland as a whole. The foundation of this will be guided by the vision that everybody has access to a good quality, affordable and sustainable home that is appropriate for their needs and is located within a thriving and inclusive community, and the work and focus of the Housing Executive in Northern Ireland will be key to the realisation of any such future.

Community led housing is being considered here as an option, and Cohousing proposals are emerging, with two schemes – one in Portaferry and another in Belfast – currently seeking sites for their developments. See www.portaferrycohousing.org/ www.cohousingconnections.org/ Support is also available for other 'co-operative' ventures (www.coopalternatives.coop) and to assist with the potential transfer of public lands or property (www.dtni.org.uk).

Wales

Cohousing opportunities in Wales have been modest to date. The principal advocate for co-op and Cohousing projects is Cwmaps, formerly the Wales Co-operative Centre (Canolfan Cydweithredol). Cwmpas runs the Communities Creating Homes programme as the CLH-Hub for community-led housing in Wales: www.cwmpas.coop/what-we-do/services/co-operative-community-led-housing

There is one completed Cohousing scheme in Wales, currently registered with the UK Cohousing Network: Dôl Llys in Llanidloes, Powys – an ex-care home which was converted into dwellings and associated facilities in 1992. Several other projects are in the early stages of development and there is clear evidence of demand for this type of neighbourhood development. Of note is a co-developed project to implement Cohousing for older people in Torfaen which is being run by Cwmpas alongside the local housing association, Bron Afon, with funding from the UK Small Business Research Initiative (results due 2023).

Groups need to be aware of specific Welsh legislation, such as the One Planet Development Act 2010 that provides a way for people to obtain planning permission to live and work on their own land, as long as there will be measurable economic, environmental and social benefits. Residents are required to meet their basic household needs from their land-based activity within five years. Subject to these strict environmental conditions, housing developments linked to using land productively can be built in 'open country'. This can enable people to buy land for housing purposes at agricultural rates, and a handful of groups have developed rural communal housing schemes, whilst others are considering cohousing projects. Wales' ageing population means that the benefits from Cohousing for older people is likely to be a welcome offer when its benefits are better understood by local authorities and registered social landlords. Cwmpas has identified several ways to help Cohousing interests in Wales:

- Increase outreach to explain the benefits to communities and key decision-makers

- Build support in local authorities, housing associations and private developers

- Integrate Cohousing ideas with use of local technologies such as timber materials

- Work with the Welsh Government to create new funding streams for CLH projects

- Work with Planning Aid Wales to create a planning guide for community groups

- Provide training to develop the skills and abilities of community groups

- Integrate the promotion of Cohousing principles with wider policy objectives set down in the Wellbeing of Future Generations Act and similar legislation.

LILAC Cohousing, Yorkshire

Building the group

The first stage of a project is to build up initial membership of a group, give it legal status and agree its vision for living in a shared neighbourhood.

The term 'group' denotes the formative phase in which a Cohousing project's members first come together and establish their common vision. This terminology is taken from the 'CLH project pipeline' promoted by Community Led Homes, the national alliance of community-led housing organisations, and reflects the CLH sector's 'pipeline' framework incorporated into this Guide.

Any Cohousing project will require continual engagement by its members throughout all stages of its development. Even where external partners are engaged to provide key services, a group's own activities must continue throughout the whole project.

The list below shows the main phases of a project's development but it should not be read as an absolute linear order in which to undertake tasks; groups will usually need to work on more than one task at a time.

Understanding the basics

What is Cohousing, exactly?

This Guide is compiled for groups who have already decided that they wish to create the Cohousing ideal. It may take a few discussions before group members feel confident that they share a common sense of what 'Cohousing' represents, and what it will represent for them.

Cohousing projects have:

● all decisions taken under the control of their residents;

● neighbourhood designs that maximise the social and shared contact between residents;

● self-contained accommodation, plus significant common facilities and spaces;

● a size and scale appropriate to underpinning the sustainable neighbourhood dynamics.

In exploring the fundamentals of how to establish a new Cohousing project, it is important to recognise that this is a model for creating a neighbourhood, and a neighbourhood's way of life, not just a 'housing' project – even one shared by the residents. Cohousing is a focus on an area, and on the relationships that can be fostered within the area by its dwellings, its other buildings and facilities, its open and shared spaces and, crucially, by people's common intent.

The importance that Cohousing gives to its size and scale, and how this impacts on its neighbourhood dynamics, is a crucial feature that is not always well understood in the UK. All new project groups will need to think through how to get the best out of whatever place they will use for their homes in order to achieve their vision. The DESIGN section of this Guide gives further information on this key point.

Is it for everyone?

Cohousing, as a particular form of neighbourhood initiative, represents a firm challenge to conventional housing development. It is not a means to build speculatively, filling a site with as many units as the housing market can absorb, but neither is it automatically a form of 'social housing', though members might hope that it could embrace or provide some social housing units in the fullness of time.

Few households have experienced collaboration in creating a more deliberate and styled environment for a home. Such a collective endeavour – deciding, agreeing and working on a common goal together with others – is not an experience that many people have had in their private lives. Cohousing will inevitably test whether households have the personal persistence and flexibility needed to identify others with a similar intent, establish ways to work together, and then be prepared for the extended length of time that it will take to achieve the common goal that the group has set for itself.

Can a site come before a group?

A place for a potential Cohousing project could be identified by a promoter of such ideas (a landowner or a developer) before a group has been formed, but around which a project could be established. This would clearly be a positive focus around which interested households could come together.

The requirements for a new project to consolidate how it could operate as a collective force, and how it could work with external partners (like the property owner) would still apply, but having a potential site there for the taking would certainly save some time and effort!

Key Books

Aside from film-based sources of information and inspiration, there are myriad reports and academic works that have examined Cohousing from many different angles, and some very instructive books (see Resources section at the end of this Guide):

The introductory parts to 'Cohousing: A Contemporary Approach to Housing Ourselves' and 'Creating Cohousing: Building Sustainable Communities' by Kathryn McCamant and Charles Durrett, and 'The Senior Cohousing Handbook' by Charles Durrett are brilliant depictions of what Cohousing represents, both in Europe and in North America. As core introductions to Cohousing's characteristics and achievements these are simply essential reading!

Useful advice for starting new Cohousing projects can be found in works like the 'Cohousing Handbook: Building a Place for Community' from Chris Hanson in the US, and in 'CoHousing Inclusive' from Germany. A good summary of Cohousing projects around the world is provided in 'Living Together – Cohousing ideas and Realities Around the World', which talks about experiences pooled at an international gathering a few years ago.

The few publications that are specific to the UK include 'Thinking about Cohousing' by Martin Field and 'Cohousing in the UK' from the Diggers and Dreamers Collective. Both describe what distinguishes Cohousing projects from other community and housing initiatives. Publications are also now available on the detailed development of specific projects, like 'Low Impact Living: A Field Guide to Ecological, Affordable Community Building' from Paul Chatterton, which describes the LILAC project in Leeds – or on specific themes, such as Maria Brenton's 'We're in Charge: Cohousing Communities of Older People in the Netherlands – Lessons for Britain?'

Videos

It will be important for any new group to establish quickly what its new members share as an understanding of what Cohousing projects have created and what they include. Some useful starting points are to watch a few video presentations together and to share information from the Cohousing literature. A set of helpful introductory pieces from specific UK projects such as those listed below are also available and can offer the opportunity to compare examples together:
cohousing.org.uk/information/videos/#what-is-cohousing

This list includes some 'TED' talks such as one on the core concepts and practice of Cohousing:
www.youtube.com/watch?v=ef9azOeuCPY

Pieces from specific UK projects that can offer the opportunity to compare examples together, such as those from:

- LILAC in Yorkshire
- Springhill in Gloucestershire
- Forgebank in Lancashire
- Chapeltown in Yorkshire

An extensive list of videos on Cohousing projects for older households has been produced by New Ground (Older Women's Cohousing Group) and is available online at:
cohousing.org.uk/information/videos/#owch-women

KEY MESSAGE
The founding
momentum behind
a new project
could start from
a collection of
individuals sharing
ideas, or from a
local supporter
with a potential si...
to use.

Finance Design Live Build Group

How should we start a group?

Feeling comfortable with a shared vision of Cohousing does not automatically mean that the potential members of a Cohousing group know the best ways to establish a new group or understand the best ways for it to work.

Engaging with others because you share Cohousing values is the first step in creating an organisation that can deliver a complex project in an organised and democratic way. Establishing a new group to progress a communal project is not a common experience, so it is understandable if people feel uncertain about how to proceed.

The habits established by a new group at its beginning can have long-reaching consequences, so if a central aim of a new Cohousing group is to establish a new neighbourhood with a shared ethos in which everyone is considered equal, then it is important that the founding members of the group are committed to this approach. Hence, if the project is to be a mixed-tenure scheme then it is important to include people who represent the different tenures in the group at the earliest stage, so that these different viewpoints are built into the decision-making practice of the group.

The long-term formalities needed for groups to establish themselves as legal entities are noted in the sub-section on 'legal identities' below. In the short-term, groups need to establish their own procedures for reaching decisions.

● Majority voting is the method most people are familiar with, but groups will need to decide for themselves whether voting 'rights' are given to individuals or to households.

Sometimes projects give more than one vote to each household, knowing that two adults in the same household may not always vote for the same outcome!

● A lot of Cohousing groups use consensus decision-making. This approach has been described as 'a system of governance which seeks to create harmonious social environments and productive organisations' [www.sociocracy.co.uk]. A short guide to consensus decision-making can be found at www.seedsforchange.org.uk/shortconsensus

Majority voting can inadvertently create a sense of winners and losers. The bigger the decision (they will get bigger the nearer you come to living as a community), the more it can matter to people. Compromise is not always possible. For example, the question of whether a Cohousing community allows households to have pets may be a simple yes/no issue.

How can we develop our skills?

Groups may find it useful to create their own frameworks for recognising how their skills must develop during the life of their project and their activities.

A couple of previous examples of such frameworks can be found at: www.diggersanddreamers.org.uk/docs/cohousing-group-development-skills-checklist.pdf

What should we do first?

Even at an early and fairly informal stage, the group should include people who are happy to convene meetings, compile and keep track of agendas and information to share, and manage small amounts of the group's initial finances.

- *Keeping track of records such as notes of meetings or contact details will become more important once constituted.*
- *Spreading information about the project, especially on social media, is a key role that will need to be covered.*

Which of these tasks do members like doing and feel confident to do? At this stage it can be easiest if people volunteer for the tasks they feel happiest with. This need not be a stage for formal titles and elections – even if you decide you don't need a chairperson, or that you wish to rotate the role of chairing meetings, agreeing who will take a lead on some identified tasks can help avoid drift.

Project Management Tools

UKCN is aware that project management software is emerging to assist new projects. Contact UKCN for up-to-date details.

Tasks are allocated among different members of the group, with one member taking overall responsibility for project management and keeping us on track. Without him, it may well not have come so far, so quickly.
[Group in development]

As the group gets bigger, and as the project progresses, it can be useful to set up co-ordinating teams, 'start-and-finish groups', or other combinations to help share the load and involve more people. This approach can enable newcomers to get to know older members and encourage skill-sharing. Look out for opportunities such as this to draw people into joining the group and make use of their skills.

Let people use their skills – don't load onto the shoulders of those who really are uncomfortable with certain jobs
[Established community]

Decision-making

Has your group discussed how tasks and decision-making are currently shared?

Consensus decision-making is written into our articles of association, with a backstop provision to permit majority voting in case of deadlock. The articles also specify how votes are allocated in the event it goes to a vote.
[Group in development]

Do you have a plan for how to share knowledge and responsibilities between members as new people join the group?.

Bond with fun times. Keep the meetings short and sweet.
[Established community]

The whole process of working together is, in effect, a first opportunity for the group to practise what living together could represent.

KEY MESSAGE
Having a plan, and a rudimentary timetable to shape first activities, is an opportunity for a group to practice some work together before living together

Group ?

Build

Live

Finance Design

The visioning stage is a necessary chance for individuals to examine, articulate and develop their thinking and for the group to work together to agree – and adopt - the shared vision. 'Blue Sky thinking' can be creative and life enhancing - it may also be tiring. What a 'home' means to us all is intrinsically linked to our sense of ourselves, the place for our families and the kind of life we wish to have.

Many Cohousing groups start from ideas and ideals of a different way of living. Bear in mind that implementing these will be a challenge (to the group and to individuals) as well as an opportunity.

Agreeing the values and objectives of a Cohousing project is a first step towards producing a practical framework for the way a scheme could progress. This initial agreement will promote collective and democratic control of the scheme and create an immediate way for a broad range of people – beyond the project's founder members – to consider whether the project is something they would like to join.

Use an established process for community building [...] especially to discuss hopes and dreams, fears and concerns, and to get to know each other

It is important to create a simple 'vision statement' which contains the group's key aims and objectives. This vision statement can then be used:

- for informing others about the project and integrating new people into the group;

- to promote the project to key agencies whose support could be needed;

- as a point of reference throughout the life of the project, against which future choices and decisions will be assessed (internally and externally).

It feels really important to have a clear vision that everyone is committed to [but a] lot of compromise is needed and the goal of bringing the vision into being has to be worth letting go of some preferences

Think not only about the residents of your scheme but also the benefits to the neighbourhood where you will be living

New schemes now have a variety of other examples with which to compare their first thoughts for their project's values and outcomes:

Talk to existing communities about how they did it. Go and visit and ask them what has worked and what hasn't and why.

- The Threshold Centre in Dorset is a mixed tenure community combining a reused farm property with additional new dwellings.

- Forgebank in Lancaster has units in private ownership (via long leasehold) but the Cohousing body is the site freeholder and owner of the common facilities.

- Springhill (Gloucestershire), Forgebank and Cannock Mill (Essex) all have new-build dwellings (although the Common House at Cannock Mill is located in the old mill building).

- LILAC in Yorkshire is a Mutual Home Ownership (MHO) scheme for people from a range of incomes: members pay rent in accordance with individual incomes and accrue household 'equity' in the project, but all property ownership resides in perpetuity with the Cohousing organisation.

What is the group's Cohousing vision?

What are the ideas, ethics and practical outcomes that members of a Cohousing project will want to incorporate into a fundamental 'vision'?

A group can arrive at an initial vision (at least) by careful consideration of the following options...

Q1. What kind of Cohousing project do you want?

Will it be:

- an 'intergenerational/family-based' project, with a mix of household sizes, ages and compositions?
- a Senior project for older residents, established by and for households aged from 50 upwards?
- a project for a group of households operating as a 'community of interest' – such as projects being developed for a single gender (to date, these have principally been for women), or for a collection of single person households, or from a particular ethnic background?

Q2. What is the size of project you want? How many dwellings? What type? What kind of shared facilities?

The site or property that a Cohousing project finally obtains will have a huge influence on the scale of what can be created. It will, however, be sensible for projects to be as clear as possible about their initial ambitions for either:

- a small number of dwellings, within a general ethos of support and sharing between households;
- self-contained dwellings, plus Common House, plus other common and shared facilities, such as gardens, workshops, laundry, open space;
- Cohousing proposals within large or extensive neighbourhood sites that could be split into more than one appropriately-sized Cohousing community.

As noted in the section below, 'Schemes to compare with Cohousing', there is an optimum size for Cohousing projects (between 20 and 50 adults, plus children in family-based projects), and a definite range below and above which the Cohousing dynamic is unlikely to be sustained.

Q3. Do you intend to build from new, or to 'retrofit' some existing property?

There is no single approach to what buildings could be used for Cohousing projects. Cohousing outcomes can be created:

- as a completely new set of buildings and facilities, on land that was previously open or empty (either as a 'greenfield' site, or as previously used 'brownfield' land);
- as a 'retrofit' refurbishment and remodelling of existing property (like farm buildings or office buildings) or by a reorganisation and reorientation of dwellings within an existing urban area into a recognisable Cohousing 'ethos';
- as a combination of new and remodelled buildings

We are interested in Cohousing as a way of building mixed communities, with a range of different affordability levels. Why do we have such a divided housing supply, where one side is dominated by housing need/rental and the other by the market?

(Group in development)

If your vision is for something innovative, or for something you hope will be stunningly beautiful, make that as clear as you can. There is no need though to strive slavishly for something that has not been achieved before – duplicating the success of others can still be a success for you.

Groups can also consider how to broadcast their 'vision' through established channels. Local authorities have a statutory obligation to compile a register of interest from local people 'wanting to build their own homes' - and then to help find land to meet those interests. Cohousing projects can register their proposals as 'group' schemes looking to build homes for a number of members together.

What about Cohousing for older households?

There is increasing interest in Cohousing groups to develop projects for older households:

● New Ground in Barnet, London is a pioneering community initiative for older women and is a mixed tenure project for ownership and social rent.

● The Lancaster Senior Cohousing project under development will have freehold and leasehold relationships between households and the Cohousing body as freeholder, but the Cohousing body will also own the 'affordable rent' units required from this scheme.

● Cannock Mill Cohousing in Essex completed its project for single people and couples aged 50-plus in 2019. The project will accept other households as well.

● Two projects in Scotland – the Vivarium Trust in Fife and Penington Senior Cohousing – have a focus on Cohousing for older people, and Vivarium published "Cohousing – future homes for older Scots" in 2018.

There is now specific mention of 'cohousing for older people' in Government guidance on housing options for older ages – see: www.gov.uk/guidance/housing-for-older-and-disabled-people

Points to consider to make a vision for Cohousing truly inclusive

Sharing: as a basis for community led housing

Diversity: with respect to different cultures, lifestyles and to urban and rural groups

User-friendliness: having flexible processes, instead of rigid structures

Creativity: enjoyment in one's own environment and friendliness in wider participations

Focus on the common good: a non-profit orientation of housing and land resources

Complexity: removing complications from dialogue and discussions

Accessibility: an equal use and involvement in spaces and in processes

Social mix: interaction through relationships between life, work, culture and education

Ecology: a just use and inclusion of nature and edible resources

Co-operation: exchanges between housing initiatives, social agencies and local authorities

Long-term planning: sustainable inclusivity, instead of short-term problem-solving

Learning: experimental and innovative self-organised projects

(Adapted from "Cohousing Inclusive: community-led housing for all', Institute for Creative Sustainability, Berlin, 2017)

Will the property 'ownership' be mainly individual home ownerships, or will there be a common or mutual ownership of the property by the group's members as a whole?

- In some Cohousing projects, individual households have an 'ownership' of their own homes, with properties being bought and sold through the housing market (albeit at times under terms and conditions laid down by the Cohousing group).
- Other projects look to distribute the economic benefits of the scheme more equitably between all members through a form of a 'Mutual Home Ownership' arrangement.
- In some cases, a mix of ownership types may be appropriate, with some units owned by individual households and others retained collectively by the Cohousing organisation to rent out to members.

Some Cohousing projects start with a very strong desire to create ecologically, as well as socially, sustainable schemes. There are a number of environmental building standards and certification schemes that groups can opt to use (see links below). All will have slightly different emphasis and benchmarks to achieve. These are applicable whether the scheme is intending to do a new build scheme or looking to retrofit existing properties. They do not replace the need to meet the minimum standards set by the statutory UK Building Regulations but act as supplementary aims for exceeding current government standards.

- AECB Building Standard and Certification www.aecb.net
- BREEAM (Building Research Establishment Environmental Assessment Method) www.breeam.com
- Passivhaus (sometimes called Passive House in the UK) standard and methodology https://www.passivhaustrust.org.uk www.leti.london/cedg

The cost of meeting any of these standards will need to be factored into a scheme's economics, alongside other affordability and financial demands.

- Will a project manager be appointed by the group to report to it?
- Will the group wish to find an 'enabling' and experienced partner to manage the project (such as a housing association or private property developer)?

The group will need to decide on what its overall role will be in the detailed development process. A group can be 'developer' and 'financier' of the project and use its own project manager to orchestrate key tasks. This way, the group takes on the risks, but it also retains control and can maximise financial economies for the group's benefit.

Another option is for a group to be the 'customer' – an external body is accepted (or engaged) as the financier and developer, and the Cohousing group is the ultimate purchaser of the built scheme and link between individual property purchases. This latter role could involve less work and potentially be less stressful, but there could also be imbalances of power between the developer and the group (as the final purchaser) if the interests of each are not in alignment.

It is inevitable that at some point there will be disagreements in the group about aspects of the development and operations of the Cohousing scheme. But when handled well, this can be constructive – both for the individuals concerned (Cohousing residents often talk about the personal growth involved in exploring differing views) and for the group, which may reach a better decision after a healthy exchange of views.

Understanding how to minimise damage to individuals and to the group at times of conflict is clearly important. The social and collective foundations a group puts in place at an early stage will be of increasing value as the project develops.

Dealing with conflict is a continuing work in progress.
[Established community]

The trickiest part is resolving conflicts. Our conflicts policy has a starting assumption that everyone is acting out of good intentions by trying to do the best for the community.
[Group in development]

A significant disagreement at an early stage in a project's life may be a necessary way that some individuals decide Cohousing is not for them after all. Significant and unresolved disagreement later on, once a scheme is on-site and money has been committed, will assume a much greater magnitude.

There is more emotion involved in Cohousing than say a CLT that is set up by local people who want to help build affordable housing for rent or shared ownership [by others] – there is more of a disconnect to the people who will live in those types of homes. I think as all the people involved in a Cohousing project are looking to be residents, then group decision-making, conflict resolution and maintaining a healthy social dynamic are challenging.
[CLH-Hub]

It is a rare group that will not benefit from using examples and experience of other projects as material to help them consider how they should organise themselves. Some groups deliberately seek external advice and even training to help establish suitable habits. Sources of such advice are extensive. Some examples that have been used to help compile this Guide are::

● the Seeds for Change website seedsforchange. org.uk has a mass of useful resources and publishes a handbook on consensus decision-making and provides training for groups;

● publications like 'the Empowerment Manual: A Guide for Collaborative Groups', which contains some powerful case histories and illustrative stories of community projects plus written exercises to help groups hone their collaborative skills;

● the Community Led Homes website (H);

● Wrigleys Solicitors – long term supporters of the community led housing sector – who supply more information on tackling decision-making at: www.wrigleys.co.uk/news/community-led-housing/cohousing-communications-conflicts-and-developing-an-effective-governance-framework

● Anthony Collins Solicitors – guidance for co-operatives, social enterprises, values-driven businesses and community organisations

Be mindful to have some degree of a 'fall-back' position on the core issues that a group considers to be crucially important, to be adopted as a final resort. As one group highlighted, 'don't let the perfect get in the way of accepting what's still good...!

How will new members learn about the work you have done and the decisions made, to lessen the chances of conflict in the future?

Spend some time in meals together from the start – you can learn a lot about people in those informal, relaxed moments over the washing up or making coffee. Go for walks or pub outings or bring-and-share in each other's homes.
[Group in development]

Points for your group to note and decide:

It's up to you to decide how much time to spend on 'decision-making' methods at this stage. Some groups spend a long time (and in some cases a lot of money) on facilitated sessions, awaydays, etc. Others may decide not to invest significant time or money until the project becomes more real, such as when a potential site is identified or secured.

As a minimum, it's important to gain a shared awareness of the choices around decision-making and to come to an agreement about how to make decisions.

Some projects plan their key discussions and items to debate at least two meetings in advance – one to review the topic (and any choices to be considered), the next to reach an agreement.

The process isn't linear. There will be a reward from maintaining a constant focus on improving the group's processes and how it can include its members in key discussions throughout all stages of a project's development.

We adopted Sociocracy for our organisational structure and decision-making... We have found it serves our needs very well and enables us to encourage every member to voice their views, and to make satisfactory decisions even when we start from a position where members hold diametrically opposed opinions.
[Group in development]

WHERE CAN WE LEARN MORE?

As a group, inform yourselves about the options. Videos you could watch as a group and other useful resources include:

About consensus decision-making:
- *www.cohousing.org.uk/wiki-categories/webinars/*
- *www.cohousing.org.uk/product/building-united-judgement/*

More information about sociocracy here:
- *www.sussexcohousing.org.uk/single-post/2016/06/10/Our-decision-making-processes*
- *www.communityledhomes.org.uk/resource/introduction-sociocracy*
- *www.sociocracyforall.org*

And some reading:
- *Briefing sheet about decision-making at LILAC:*
  www.communityledhomes.org.uk/resource/community-briefing-sheet
- *Information on Cannock Mill's method of working together, including a link to their decision-making process:*
  www.cannockmillcohousingcolchester.co.uk/work/

Who can help us?

Groups need to think through whether they will look for external support to help mould their initial ideas into a cohesive focus. Not all groups will feel they have the capacities and skills to deal with the initial tasks that projects must address. Having an external and experienced point of contact from whom a project can take advice and informed opinion will be a valuable support in itself. In more practical ways, external skills can also help a Cohousing project:

● submit applications for funds to help with capacity-building in the group's formative period;

● consolidate new decision-making and governance procedures;

● confirm the Cohousing vision;

● consider what kind of development partnerships could be required in due time;

● undertake initial appraisals of potential sites;

● produce an appropriate business plan for the proposed projections.

There is a role for a social enabler to manage communication between the Cohousing community and professionals.
[CLH Hub]

Some groups may be able to apply for 'start-up' grants, which could then be used to pay the first fees of Hubs or Facilitators. Groups which are planning to progress through a primarily through use of their members' private resources may require members to each contribute an initial sum that can be used for external professional support in the early stages of the project.

Will people understand what we want?

If new Cohousing projects are uncertain or unused to thinking of where to turn for assistance, they can consider contracting some initial services from the local Community Led Housing Hub (CLH-Hub). These have been established across the country to assist community-led housing schemes. Some Hubs employ their own personnel and co-ordinate the engagement of semi-independent CLH Facilitators (who have achieved accreditation from Community Led Homes).

Cohousing groups can find the local CLH-Hub by using the search facility on the Community Led Homes website: **www.communityledhomes.org.uk**

See the SITE section for further information. It is never too early for a group to consider engaging its own project manager, who can act as a prominent advocate in negotiations and meetings with other partners.

Cannock Mill Cohousing, Essex

Advice to groups

Professionals from a variety of backgrounds could have useful experience to support Cohousing projects, but this will need to be investigated by each project group. The kinds of skills likely to be attractive to community-led housing and Cohousing projects will be those required to undertake community-building and property development; they could also extend to assisting with individual and collective control over future housing operations and tenures.

Some architectural firms have a track record of working with designs for community projects; some workers employed by existing 'community anchor' bodies (which may already exist in the local voluntary sector) can be familiar with helping new community projects start, from the bottom up. The following roles are ones that Hubs and other Facilitators are being commissioned to provide (as listed by one of the regional CLH-Hubs):

- assess and provide guidance on initial community-led housing proposals;
- assist the set-up and running of steering groups and boards of directors/ trustees;
- provide guidance and training to communities on developing good governance and legal models;
- explain community-led housing to communities through presenting case studies and arranging visits;
- signpost groups to start-up and specialist grants and assist with grant applications;
- provide template documents and guidance on good practice;
- support communities and local authorities to consider flexible use of planning policies like rural exception sites;
- advise on how to evidence local housing demands through housing need surveys;
- assist with the development of community membership schemes;
- assist with community consultations and community engagement;
- guide land searches and assessments, and assist with landowner negotiations;
- lead on project management and the use of scheme resources;
- assist/lead on business plan preparation and scheme appraisals;
- help identify and introduce project delivery partners (appropriate for the development model chosen);
- guide on key professional appointments e.g. solicitor, architect, employers' agent etc;
- provide projects with support throughout the local design and planning process;
- provide guidance and support to housing management and maintenance roles.

 KEY MESSAGE
The kinds of skills likely to be attractive to community led housing and Cohousing projects will be from professionals able to provide advocacy and support for community-building and for property development

Building and rebuilding the membership

Group members

Membership building and re-building is an ongoing task. The progress of a Cohousing development can take substantial time, and the project's membership will undoubtedly undergo some change, whether between members who are or are not interested in a certain site, or from an influx of new interest once a potential site has been identified. New and prospective members need a firm understanding of what the project will offer them, however much (or little) they are actively involved in its developmental stages.

There is a role here for a 'members prospectus' or 'statement of intent' that gives a concise summary of what the scheme is focused on and of what it offers to, and requires from, its members as tasks progress. This could also summarise the project's constitutional set-up, its decision-making process, the way it will be financed, and how it will govern the allocation of completed units in the finished scheme. An example document is available at: www.vivariumtrust.scot/members/

Inclusivity

The success of Cohousing projects, locally and nationally, will be in how well their make-up and membership reflects that of the wider community.

A Cohousing project which doesn't reflect its surrounding neighbourhood would stand out like a sore thumb.

[Cohousing group member]

It will be crucial to recruit members from a broad set of backgrounds as early as possible.

See the DIVERSITY & INCLUSION pages and further information in the RESOURCES section.

A number of projects have started in which the first households have been those who have their own financial resources or independence and who may feel it straightforward to give time and energy to the project's gestation. Other groups have started with initial members from a range of economic backgrounds but have struggled to secure engagement from households whose personal circumstances have meant any 'ownership' tenures will be unaffordable to them.

Whether a Cohousing project intends to provide a future mix of housing tenures (i.e. with 'ownership' options and 'affordable' options) or a 'Mutual Home Ownership' arrangement, having the right mix of households involved at its heart through all stages of its development is crucial. The joint working that takes place in the early stages can underpin the community's identity and dynamic together as it grows.

Prospective members of any 'affordable' housing could be initially identified through a general agreement between the Cohousing project and the local authority to seek interest from households already identified as in need of future housing on the statutory housing register (i.e. those on the council's 'housing waiting list'), or from tenants of social housing who may be keen to move into the Cohousing project on completion.

Groups could negotiate with the local authority about ways to identify households from suitable backgrounds and ways for them to demonstrate a commitment to the Cohousing ideals and vision (another reason for agreeing these and writing them down!).

Responding to general enquiries

A group needs to be clear on how it will respond to enquiries once it has broadcast its ideas and proposals. It is important to identify who will take the lead on co-ordinating this so that enquiries and prospective members don't fall through the net.

Once the first members have initiated and discussed some ideas, the group needs to plan how it will respond to enquiries about its identity and its scope – and at what point it feels ready to go public.

> *A group of friends formed the initial core group. In the early days three public events were held. We are now members of UK Cohousing and can be contacted via their website. We have a website, Facebook and Twitter accounts, and have received some enquiries through these. We distribute flyers and business cards at various networking events for age-friendly and community-led housing.*
>
> *[Group in development]*

Some meetings (probably not all) of the core group will merit being 'open' to people who have heard about the scheme and who wish to explore whether they might be interested in becoming future members and residents. A big part of this will be through the original members informing newcomers at the outset of the work done so far and what the group may already be committed to – for example, if there is already a particular style of collective decision-making.

> *[We] established a 'newcomers' procedure, initially coordinated by a membership and community building action group.*
>
> *[Established community]*

A 'membership scheme' or set of procedures will enable groups to keep in touch with interested people, whether they are ready to become more active or not. A key role here is membership secretary, whose job will be to keep records up to date and to make sure everyone is kept informed.

> *[We have] a membership secretary who follows up all enquiries to our email address, sending out an information pack which is updated regularly. If they are interested after reading the pack they can have an informal meet-up with members. We are about to set up a website.*
>
> *[Group in development]*

Wider meetings to share information about the project's ambitions and progress can inform and update others on the project's key ideas and 'sell' the idea of Cohousing as the fundamental concept. Such meetings could also include a speaker from the local CLH-Hub or from an established Cohousing scheme if there is one nearby.

Prospective members

Does a project need a 'waiting list' for its members? Probably not in its formative stages. Most projects experience a period when they must continue publicising their project in order to find sufficient future members and occupants. The exception could be where there are already sufficient initial members to fill the planned number of dwellings. In that instance, the initial members may wish to limit future entrants into a 'full' membership, in order to make sure they receive a firm offer of a home in the future development themselves.

During its formative years, New Ground in Barnet, London (originally known as OWCH – the 'Older Women's Cohousing Project') gained a substantial number of interested households and formed a waiting list even before the project was built. Prospective members were encouraged to participate in the group's activities, both to demonstrate their longstanding interest in the project and for the project to learn more about them as time went by. Future occupiers could then be found or selected with some familiarity to the community.

Some groups have also recognised that they felt a little 'swamped' in their early stages when their meetings had a number of 'one-off' or casual attendeees, and so choose to separate more business-focused meetings of core members from more general 'visitor' meetings.

Cohousing groups running projects which offer 'affordable units' in particular may want to consider keeping a waiting list from which to identify future occupants of any vacated units. Groups may feel they want specific criteria to apply to finding such households, even though this could require negotiation with the local authority. Most local authorities are used to procedures for allocating households from the housing register to any available dwellings, but their usual procedures may not be the best way to find households that really want to be part of a Cohousing community. Creative responses to such matters have, however, been used by many housing co-operatives with similar concerns, so there are clear precedents within the social housing environment for such arrangements

The Cohousing group can also point out that property vacated elsewhere by existing social tenants – vacated in order for them to come to the Cohousing neighbourhood – will become available to other households in need of such rental accommodation. In this way, the Cohousing project would continue to help meet the wider needs of households in need.

Project supporters

Not everyone who expresses interest and comes to a Cohousing meeting will become a resident. Information about the project will need to be structured so that it can inform a variety of local interests and potential partners, including the wider community close to where a Cohousing development might take place.

It could be worth thinking about creating categories of membership to keep people in touch and to facilitate a request for support at various points (lobbying local Councillors at the appropriate time, for example).

Publicity

The publicity material a project produces will be a test of (and testament to) its vision. Its members will want all of this to be clear, inspiring and easy to understand.

Use the vision statement to inform the project's website, Facebook, Twitter feeds and any other social media content.

Use existing networks, personal contacts and local groups interested in community-led housing, self-build, etc as well as other groups like U3A and UK Cohousing Network, which send out newsletters.

Produce materials that are easy to distribute, like a flyer to give out at appropriate local events, or small notices that can be placed on noticeboards, in shop windows, etc.

Develop a brief presentation (perhaps on PowerPoint) that can be used at local events to introduce the idea of Cohousing to potential members and/or supporters and to summarise the project's ideals.

[We] built a website early on and set up Facebook and Twitter accounts. We have struggled with using social media and our website for marketing, despite some short-term assistance from Reach volunteers [... but also] reached out through local media, including local radio.

Host events with a local and 'community' focus that could engage the kind of households sought by the scheme – such as family-oriented fun events, or shared community meals and 'pot-luck' dinners in a local venue.

Use work and faith networks – it may be possible to advertise news about the project via community and faith networks and via employers or trade unions.

Note that as the scheme progresses, you will need to produce material targeted at would-be residents informing them of more detail – your constitutional set-up, your decision-making process and how you intend to finance the scheme as that all becomes clearer.

Building from diverse backgrounds

Why Diversity?

Diversity is responsible for creating our amazing complex planet. The very differences that we shun, avoid, or even destroy are necessary for life to continue in a multitude of magnificent forms. This does not mean it is easy to embrace or even understand diversity, but it is a precious necessity.

[Cohousing stakeholder, USA]

UKCN's visions is for all citizens and groups to be able to set up Cohousing communities and neighbourhoods should they wish to. Cohousing is about creating environments in which people feel that they belong – inclusive, open environments in which diversity is embraced and differences are valued. People should feel confident in being themselves and in having their differences in identity and thought respected, creating a culture of fairness and opportunity.

Older generations often struggle to find identity except by opposition and exclusion. In contrast, younger generations have grown up being connected to the world through the internet and social media, [and] largely accept diversity as the normal way of life. By 2030 over 60% of urban populations will be under the age of 18. So, what if we began to develop a way of thinking where difference was seen as a gift rather than a threat?

[UKCN diversity working group]

Diversity and inclusion are not problems to be solved or divisions to be overcome but can be seen as fundamental to the very heart of life itself. Working to increase diversity and social inclusion can help both Cohousing communities and the organisations that support them realise their values more effectively.

We didn't think about diversity until quite late on, at which point we were under pressure to find enough buyers in time, when it became a question of prioritising who had the money to move in rather than the nature of the community we were creating.

[Established community]

Far too often diversity and inclusion are seen as compliance issues – 'something that we have to do' – rather than as elements of a vibrant and sustainable community. The pursuit of diversity can actually strengthen the sustainability of community housing though. So the Cohousing movement has every reason to truly celebrate and value diversity in all its forms.

Aspects of Diversity

In the UK, marginalised communities are least able to access affordable housing, and a considered approach to diversity and inclusion can help to address disadvantage.

[CEO, Housing Diversity Network]

Many people think of diversity as relating to aspects such as ethnicity, sexuality, gender and (dis)ability. To be truly diverse and inclusive, many other aspects should also be taken into consideration. These include wealth, class, education, literacy, age, familiarity with digital technology and fluency in English.

Embracing diversity does not mean compromising on important criteria for membership, however. Groups with shared values around sustainability, equality, participation and sharing, for example, may turn down applicants or members unwilling to live by these commitments. Values such as these are entirely complementary to a conscious approach to diversity and inclusion.

It can be helpful to approach diversity through the lens of the different identities we have and how they weave together – sometimes called intersectionality. Our identities are not just our age, income, ethnicity, education, ability, sexuality, or culture, but are created by the combination of all these aspects together.

Some combinations might make it easier for people to become members of a specific Cohousing scheme than others. For example, a scheme might find that it easily attracts white, highly educated women who are older, have heard of Cohousing already, can downsize from the homes they already own and can afford homes at market rates.

To have a diverse community, you need to be proactive, constantly review progress and avoid complacency.

When planning outreach events for example, consider aspects of diversity such as culture and education before deciding on say, a pork-belly feast or craft beer event or opening discussions that assume that others have been to university or travelled, are political activists, or enjoy certain music. There is a lot to consider and care and attention is needed.

Even if you feel you've reached a level of diversity that you're happy with, ask a few questions to review:

- *Is your community accessible to people with different abilities?*
- *Is it affordable?*
- *Is it genuinely culturally sensitive?*

Other suggested questions are listed later.

Group **?**

Build

Live

Design

Finance

A commitment to diversity is not one-size-fits-all

Diversity can mean different things in different contexts. For example, diversity policies for a senior LGBTQ+ Cohousing scheme may look a bit different to those of a general needs Cohousing scheme which emphasises environmental sustainability or affordable housing. A Cohousing project ensuring that its residents reflect the ethnically diverse area it is in may have a different approach to achieving diversity to one located in a predominantly white area. Each Cohousing project is unique, shaped by its location and the needs, interests, resources, and values of its residents.

Developing both housing and community at the same time is a challenge. Each Cohousing community should reflect upon what diversity means within the context of their purpose and the environment they operate within, to define their policy. You may find some commitments easier to approach than others, but a genuine commitment to diversity requires an openness to explore all areas.

New Ground (also known as the Older Women's Cohousing) is a community specifically for older women but is diverse in terms of income and offers affordable social housing as well as privately owned homes. ChaCo is an intergenerational scheme in Leeds which has rigorous targets for recruiting members to ensure their scheme reflects the local population. Sturts Farm in the New Forest is committed to full equality of membership and involvement for adults described as having learning difficulties.

Maybe you've noticed unconscious bias in your intentional community. It may be there when someone on the membership committee asks: 'Is this family really a good fit for us?' or when there are more women than men in your neighbourhood but somehow meetings are mostly filled with male voices. It may be functioning when some visitors are asked questions, and others are left alone..

[Contributor, Communities Magazine]

Designing a culture of diversity: key questions to ask – 1

Creating a culture of diversity doesn't happen by accident. To make sure your Cohousing community has diversity and inclusion at its centre, ask yourselves the questions below at the various stages of development. If possible, ask a 'critical friend' to review your answers. It is not always easy to notice our own unconscious biases; constructive challenge can be very helpful to highlight our blind spots.

MEMBERSHIP

- How are your vision, values and expectations on diversity and inclusion expressed in your membership agreements?

- Where are the potential barriers to inclusion and how are you planning to address these?

- How inclusive are the designs of activities, the building, and decision-making processes?

- Who holds power in your group (both formally and informally)? Have you considered ways to acknowledge and distribute power more evenly?

- How are decisions made to ensure membership selection and onboarding processes are clear, inclusive, and transparent?

- What training and awareness-raising activities will there be relating to diversity and inclusion and how regular will they be?

- How will agreements regarding individual participation in community activities promote inclusion? How do they reflect differences in time, abilities or backgrounds or take account of changes in people's lives such as maternity, retirement, new jobs and illness?

- How will you ensure that your group is aware of the latest legal requirements on diversity and inclusion?

- How are meetings organised? Are roles such as facilitation, minutes and chairing distributed with training and support provided to take on leadership roles?

- Is attention paid to how meetings are conducted to ensure they are accessible to all members and decision-making is as simple and enjoyable as possible? Is attention paid to time, language, style, and location to ensure they are attractive and open?

- Are you celebrating diversity? Find ways to enrich the community in real, meaningful ways. Learn from each other without imposing on others.

Group

Build

Live

Finance Design

Dealing with potential bias

Is diversity and inclusion always good?

Some communities may hold a vision to support a marginalised group in a safe space, such as older people, single gender, or LGBT+ communities; others may be open to members able to meet specific requirements such as communities with an agricultural theme, where members are expected to work.

There is a difference between communities of marginalised groups carving out space for themselves in the context of isolation and discrimination in wider society and more mainstream communities that choose to benefit more privileged members of society to the exclusion of others.

> *When I moved with my family to this predominately white, progressive cohousing community, I was initially stunned by the implicit bias, microaggressions, overt acts of racism, stereotyping, and other racist and homophobic experiences we have had to overcome in order to continue living here.*
>
> *[Contributor, Communities Magazine]*

Diversity enriches communities. There are many different aspects to diversity and inclusion, and all communities should be able to consider at least some aspects within the parameters of their specific goals.

Change over time

As communities develop, their priorities may change – often due to practical considerations. For example, Cohousing groups may find it harder to attract younger people in the early years of an uncertain development journey but may then find it easier as the scheme launch date approaches when there is a much clearer offer.

To address financial inequalities, in time, Cohousing schemes launched by homeowners may seek to buy back properties and turn them into affordable rental units or peg sale prices to retain affordability in perpetuity. Communities which have addressed any issues of unconscious bias or assumptions related to race, age, (dis) ability, sexuality or class may then find a wider range of people becoming members and groups which have established inclusive decision-making processes may find a much wider range of people and voices coming to the fore.

Designing a culture of diversity: key questions to ask – 2

- Have you agreed your vision, aims and values for your Cohousing community, including outlining a position on diversity and inclusion?
- Do you have targets or measures on diversity that can be reviewed?
- Are you aware of your legal obligations regarding diversity?
- Is your group intended for a particular group or open to all?
- If your group is open to all, how will you encourage participation from sections of society which are usually under-represented in Cohousing groups?
- Do you understand the statistics for your local area? Will your community give any preference to people with strong local connections?
- Have you considered how partners such as registered housing providers and other organisations can help achieve your goals and manage allocations?

- Are your goals for diversity integrated into your advertising and recruitment processes? What steps can be taken to make them more inclusive?
- Are your communications clear about what you mean by diversity, who you are looking for and ways to engage with you?
- Are your recruitment events truly inclusive?
- How easy will it be for someone new to join your group?
- Is the tone and content of your events and messages aligned with the diversity, inclusivity and values that your community wants to develop?
- Have you checked your answers above against potential stereotypes and unconscious biases?

How should we organise... ?

New Cohousing groups will need to give careful consideration to which formal legal status is suitable for their plans and the kind of community they wish to create. A legal identity is required for a Cohousing project to have a sufficient collective entity to progress the shared ambitions and develop partnerships and plans.

'Secondary' rules will also be important to detail how members should behave in meetings and with each other. This helps to ensure that actions are taken when needed and helps avoid decision-making sessions going round in circles or being commandeered by just a small set of people.

The experience and decisions of established communities are invaluable here, even though members of new initiatives may need to be convinced that previous developments are relevant to their own situation.

When considering which legal status will best serve the community ethos, questions to take into account include:

What kind of body is best to own or possess the site on which the stated Cohousing facilities could be built?

● Would this be the same as, or different from, a legal entity that provides the dwellings to be occupied?

● What framework is best for the ownership and/or management of the Common House and other shared facilities?

● Could particular kinds of property tenure predispose a project towards one kind of legal identity rather than another?

● Can more than one kind of property tenure exist within a single legal structure?

Form should follow function. Decide what your priorities are and what you want to achieve, and only then think about what legal structure you should become... Avoid re-inventing the wheel – it is often simpler (and so cheaper) to copy what other groups have done and learn from their mistakes.
[Group in development]

There is no need here to rehearse or repeat the main information that is already available within general commentaries and advice notes on UK legal structures pertinent to each country in the UK. Groups should also be aware that not all local solicitors are as well-informed as others about the needs of community-led projects, or more specifically about structures to suit Cohousing. Advice is still encountered that does not seem to take into account the best use of conventional experience from projects elsewhere.

We were often encouraged to expect lawyers to help us make choices about legal forms, but found they were really only useful once we knew for ourselves what we wanted, and then charged a lot of money to convert our wishes into a legal form.
[Group in development]

Different legal identities will have specific requirements for annual returns to UK regulatory bodies (e.g. Companies House, Financial Conduct Authority, Community Interest Company Regulator) but this should not be seen as problematic for Cohousing members, aside perhaps from projects considering registration as a charity. Standard conditions of charitable status are that a charity's trustees should not benefit personally from the charity's endeavours – this would be extremely problematic for Cohousing members considering such a body as the vehicle to build their own homes.

Groups should contact and use the CLH-Hubs as sounding boards to help clarify initial impressions about the choice of legal identity they could make, and to think through how this will serve future operations.

A key point to keep in mind when looking at how other UK Cohousing projects are constituted is that some projects rely on individual ownership (with or without some rental properties), while others are based on 'Mutual Home Ownership', in which members have 'equity' in the scheme but the absolute property ownership remains with the mutually-based legal entity.

What forms of legal incorporation have Cohousing projects used to date?

Of the 20+ responses that were received to inform this Guide:

- two-thirds have declared themselves to have 'company' based incorporations (four of these are as a 'community interest company);
- one-third have, or intend to have, registrations as co-ops or community benefit societies;
- one organisation is a trust but is looking to develop a stand-alone Cohousing project;
- one project had yet to make a final decision on its choice of incorporation.

The Registrar of Companies for Scotland is now an official of Companies House, an Executive Agency of the United Kingdom government. To register a company in Northern Ireland, applications need to be made to Companies House, Belfast.

There are registers for charities in Scotland and Northern Ireland that are separate from registered charities in England and Wales.

The responsibility for registering mutual societies in all countries in the UK lies with the Financial Conduct Authority (FCA).

KEY MESSAGE

It will help a group to move forward if it adopts a legal format that other projects have already used in similar circumstances, rather than spending a lot of time focusing on uncertainties about its long-term identity.

Presenting the social impact of a Cohousing project

Focusing on what Cohousing projects bring to the creation of dynamic and sustainable neighbourhoods will demonstrate their wider social value.

Various assessment tools and calculators are available that attempt to measure the 'social value' of new initiatives including new housing schemes, and an increasing number of local authorities and other bodies now have their own policies on this issue. The New Economics Foundation's website (www.neweconomics.org) has useful guidance on assessing social value and the Housing Association Charitable Trust has a social value calculator for community-led housing geared around an assessment of value in using land for community benefit.

Is Cohousing good value for money?

The worth of Cohousing's outcomes and the value it has for its neighbourhoods – over and above any monetary price of the properties created – can be demonstrated in:

● creating a sense of place: how the physical design and concepts of Cohousing settings encapsulate clear community identities, with memorable buildings and spaces;

● enhanced mental and physical wellbeing: being a part of an identifiable neighbourhood community, with a shared sense of purpose and regular social contacts;

● mutually supportive communities: offering support between households in both practical and emotional ways for dealing with daily life;

● inclusive communities: showing that the community is founded on principles of inclusion and diversity and that these principles extend into its interactions with the wider area;

● empowerment of individuals: how members of Cohousing groups gain skills and confidence, throughout all phases of their communal development and life together;

● strengthening social capital and civic society: how members are more engaged and effective in wider civic society, community issues and political engagements;

● enhancement of environmental sustainability: how the physical design of Cohousing neighbourhoods supports low carbon development and community stewardship of the environment.

Laughton Lodge, Sussex

There are some important benefits for groups to consider in terms of the social value of their project. Identifying the social value that the project will achieve will::

- **link closely with fundamental Cohousing aims;**
- **help avoid 'mission drift' for what the project undertakes – so that what gets measured is what actually gets done;**
- **assist projects to make the Cohousing case more compelling to potential stakeholders and supporters..**

Ways to depict social value

In order to demonstrate a Cohousing project's social value, groups could include some of the following in a presentation:

a focus on the design quality that turns the neighbourhood scheme into more than just a housing development. See the Building For Life Guide – www.designcouncil.org.uk/resources/guide/building-life-12-third-edition

responses from members to multiple-choice questions about their experiences of Cohousing and its impact on their wellbeing;

information about how the project encourages members to participate in the Cohousing community and about ways in which members might engage in civic society at different levels.

These are some useful resources:

The annual Community Life Survey (www.gov.uk/government/collections/community-life-survey) – includes questions around subjective wellbeing which record how residents feel before and after moving in to Cohousing as well as others about social interaction, support between neighbours, and ways that members might engage in society

The annual survey of social capital published by the Office For National Statistics (www.ons.gov.uk/peoplepopulationandcommunity/wellbeing) – its content could be adapted to inform some of the above points

A guide on social value measurement from the UK Green Building Council and other information about ecological design and the planning process from the Centre for Alternative Technology (www.cat.org.uk)

KEY MESSAGE

Demonstrating the social value of Cohousing communities is not what is usually found on a standard business balance sheet

What support do groups want?

All projects will need some form of local support for their schemes, but not all groups will want support for the same kinds of things. Groups need a firm idea in their formative stage of what kinds of support are wanted from particular sources.

Is land or property to be sought from sympathetic landowners? Or from commercial interests who might be interested in some kind of two-way partnership?

Is a particular form of policy support to be sought from the local authority, that can support the formal approvals for future neighbourhood designs, or for inclusion of 'affordable housing'?

Is professional and managerial support sought to assist or mentor a group to undertake the detailed development tasks?

Does the group want a more enabling form of support from a site developer who can be more formally engaged to develop a scheme on their behalf?

Is the group looking for a partnership with an external body to help meet planning obligations for 'affordable housing' units, especially the kind of body that could contribute finance, loans or a grant?

When talking to external stakeholders and potential supporters, a Cohousing group will want to discuss those bodies' support for:

● projects with a collective intent to stimulate a shared and sustainable neighbourhood life;

● projects that reflect the identity and diversity of the communities being proposed and which are socially and economically inclusive;

● projects that combine the best ideas for and experience of shaping domestic spaces and places, both in individual dwellings and through mutually-shared 'common' facilities;

● projects that can maximise the potential in sites or property that those external bodies may be able to provide or help the group to acquire.

East Whins, Moray

Will the council help us?

Support to any project from its local authority will be an enormous lift to a group's ambitions, whether that be at the level of elected Councillors, through its paid officers, or in its regulatory functions (like its role as a local planning authority). Building a positive relationship with the authority is an essential element in a group consolidating its early confidence, and an invaluable asset when the proposals are judged by third-party interests and by prospective members.

It's a long road.
A supportive local authority is vital to make early progress.

But... do not assume there will be immediate support for a project to create a new neighbourhood of 20-30 properties – for many local authorities, a substantially-sized project, steered by a group for its own members, will be something new.

Do not assume either that specific ideas about Cohousing will be understood immediately – some authorities may interpret all 'community-led housing' projects as being basically similar, yet their prior experience may be of something else that does not yet understand Cohousing's key characteristics...

Site investigations have provided valuable learning and helped develop contacts with local Councillors and officials. Get to know your local planning department and ensure your local authority understands what Cohousing and community-led housing is [sic].

Marmalade Lane Cohousing, Cambridgeshire

Local authorities, housing associations and developers

The bodies in the local authority (public) sector with whom new projects will need to have contact include:

- City councils (in the larger urban areas)

- Borough and district councils (in smaller and rural authority areas)

- Parish and town councils (at local levels, with junior roles subservient to the districts in which they are based)

- other bodies in designated areas, such as the planning authorities with responsibilities in National Parks or other places of 'outstanding natural beauty'.

All these statutory bodies are used to responding to initial ideas for new housing provision, both of the potential use of sites or reuse of available property or for what could be created to meet established local priorities. They are less used to having substantial new developments being brought forward by community projects and groups themselves and may need some encouragement to see the all-round positive values that Cohousing represents.

The external interests in the broader housing and development sectors that new projects could wish to contact include:

- housing associations/registered providers;

- housebuilders or constructors (principally in the private sector);

- housing developers (also in the private sector) and land or property owners.

- the grant-making agencies within each country that govern the use and investment of housing development finances from the public purse.

The phrase 'RSL' (registered social landlord) ceased to be the technical term some years ago... [we] suggest using the phrase 'registered providers (RP), such as housing associations' a couple of times and then revert to 'housing association', or 'housing association/other RP'

[CLH-Hub]

Most of these bodies will be used to organising and managing new housing and neighbourhood development proposals for themselves – which may be the key reason why some groups hope to identify one that could be interested in supporting their Cohousing ideas and taking on the bulk of the development responsibilities!

Projects seeking 'enabling' support from external partners should use a formal Memorandum of Understanding or Heads of Terms agreement as a basis for what such a partnership will entail.

What groups will need to provide will be cogent ideas for how their own project can be made understandable to bodies from external backgrounds, and to how any level of participation in future work together could be professionally and economically attractive.

The kind of initial support and services that a group may seek from the local CLH-Hub or Facilitators could certainly include guidance on how to focus approaches to any of these external bodies.

Examples of proposals to use funds from private or public sources are given in the FINANCE section of this Guide.

Finding 'enabling' developers

Groups can certainly benefit from establishing partnerships with supportive developers (especially if a partner has a site to use), just as developers can benefit from the kudos that a successful project can bring to their own reputation and from the guaranteed custom that a project's members represent on completion.

Identifying that right blend of experience and support will be a key task. When your group is considering whether to go into partnership with an external body like a housing association or property developer, the following questions could be discussed with them:

1. What is their understanding or familiarity with 'Cohousing' neighbourhoods and ideas?

2. Have they any experience of working with a Cohousing project or other community-led housing project? (If 'yes', ask for details.)

3. What would motivate the partner to support the project?

4. Have they involved prospective resident households in the development of previous housing/neighbourhood projects? (If 'yes', ask for details.)

5. Have they got any experience of working to deliver mixed-income/mixed-tenure initiatives? (If 'yes', ask for details.)

6. What resources or expertise would they bring to the proposed project? (Land? Finances? Other contacts?)

7. Would the organisation engage with the project if it was managed by another body (such as by the Cohousing group or its own project manager)?

8. Would key personnel be available for meetings at evenings or weekends, if required?

9. What would be the basis of the partner's future cost or fees, or of another form of financial return they might want from the project? When would money be required for them?

Threshold Centre

KEY MESSAGE

Groups should be clear about their ideas of what support they want from external partners before approaching them. Projects wanting an 'enabling' and experienced external partner to manage the project's development (like a housing association or private property developer) need a clear Memorandum of Agreement for what is desired and offered within such a partnership.

Group

Build

Live

Design

Finance

CLH Facilitators and Hubs could support projects in the Group stage through:.

Facilitation

Providing supportive facilitation to new projects in their formative 'start-up' period

Legal Incorporation

Giving information on the use and role of different legal incorporations

Applications

Helping with compiling and submitting applications for start-up funds

Support

Support for a project's 'Visioning' and its formation of an initial 'Cohousing Prospectus'.

Assistance

Helping groups structure the way they compile submissions for assistance and support to local authorities and stakeholders

Presentation

Supporting groups to compile the text and presentational format about themselves looking for a suitable site

Our Hub is made up of local authority officers; we can explain the process of acquiring council-owned land and buildings

[CLH-Hub]

Shaping

Supporting projects to shape themselves to be policy-compliant in achieving mixed local housing provisions and delivering affordable units within more holistic neighbourhoods

Social value

Helping to compile social value presentations and to lobby for the release of public land for projects with such positive values.

Key stakeholders (for example local government authorities; second-tier town, parish and community councils; housing associations; developers; etc.) could support projects in the GROUP stage through:

Develop community-led policy

Developing policy support for neighbourhood developments that want to create places with lasting social value

Start-up support

Supporting the provision of 'start-up' grants to new projects

Membership of community groups

Helping Cohousing projects identify potential members for future 'affordable' units at the earliest stage, in order to participate in all the project's development tasks and stages

Sale or transfer of land and property

Adopting asset disposal policies to direct the use of land or redundant buildings to Cohousing and other CLH schemes

Design codes

Adopting local design codes that can support Cohousing's focus on size and scale and placement of buildings on-site

Planning designations

Confirming that a 'Common House' and similar shared facilities are extensions of domestic space and do not need a separate planning designation

Exception sites

Offering flexibility with rural 'exception site' policies where Cohousing schemes can provide benefits to the wider local community

Forgebank Cohousing, Lancashire

Finding the site

This section of the Guide is to help group members in their search for suitable land or for a property that can be remodelled to meet the needs of their project.

Central to the outcome here will be obtaining the right opportunity to create the size of neighbourhood that members aspire to have, and for that neighbourhood to have the key facilities that underpin the identity of a Cohousing community.

Different systems of property law operate in the different countries within Great Britain. In England, Wales and Northern Ireland the two commonly encountered types of land ownership are freehold (where the property is owned outright and is not time-limited) and leasehold (where there is an exclusive right to occupy the property for a set period of time). In Scotland, the equivalent to "freehold" would be "heritable" interest – whilst there is a concept of leasehold ownership, legislation has been passed which has converted certain ultra-long leases (with an initial term of more than 175 years and an annual rent of £100 or less) into heritable title (outright ownership). A lease can be for up to 999 years. Buying the property means buying the right to live there for the duration of the lease. There is, however, usually an annual charge for leasehold properties – known as 'ground rent' - paid to the person or body who owns the land. Established cohousing schemes have used both of these forms of ownership for their projects.

Useful overviews of comparative property terms and concepts across England and Scotland can be found at these sites: www.dentons.com and www.shepwedd.com (search: differences between English and Scottish property law)

Locating a suitable site, or finding vacant buildings that can be remodelled or extended, is the perennial issue that confronts Cohousing projects. Much time can be consumed in hoping that a feasible and available site will emerge that a group can secure, or that a sympathetic landowner can be found to support the group's neighbourhood ambitions.

The 'site' seems to be the biggest stumbling block of almost all Cohousing groups... [although] groups sometimes have unrealistic expectations of the site they can achieve at the cost they can afford.
[CLH-Hub]

This view from the experience of the CLH-Hubs has recognised the different scale of challenge that Cohousing projects present compared with other community-led initiatives.

We are trying to set up Coho of 20 – 40 units with mixed tenure in one of the most expensive cities in the country. There is a lot of difference [... to...] setting up on a large plot bought outright in a cheaper city.
[Oxford CLH]

For the majority of Cohousing groups, there will not be any escape from a long and continuous contact with external bodies and interests which could offer a route to finding a suitable location, including:

- the property or estates officers and elected members inside the local authority responsible for holding and managing the council's assets;

- similar officers in other public sector bodies, like hospital trusts, responsible for their asset management strategies and disposals;

- private sector property developers and housebuilders, the largest of whom can hold massive stocks of land for housebuilding purposes (called 'land-banks'), but who have minimal experience of sharing this with community projects;

- other local landowners and smaller housebuilders, who often have more localised parcels of land, and who could be interested in the local building services being commissioned to build properties to a group's instructions;

- other housing bodies, such as established housing associations and newer 'registered providers', more of whom are themselves finding land to acquire and hold in their own land-banks, and who are likely to have at least some history of providing housing services for the local community.

Compile a formal summary

Groups will find it worthwhile to compile a formal summary of the land or property they are seeking and to phrase it within an engaging description of the kind of development they would like to create.

For many external organisations who are not familiar with group-led projects, or community-led ones, it can be easy to imagine that 'Cohousing' is odd or alternative, or that it is strange and unrealistic. A think-tank report in 2015 reported views from a local village that the idea of deliberately creating a housing scheme where people might want to eat meals together seemed very odd (if not unpalatable!); Cohousing groups should anticipate that first proposals can sometimes receive a mixed reception.

Some groups have engaged local land or property agents to locate suitable and affordable sites on which a new Cohousing project could be based. Given that this could be for an indeterminate length of time, a contractual arrangement could be better tied to results (actually finding a suitable option or two) rather than being engaged for a fixed period.

Local property auctions are also a way of finding out about potential land or property, though a group may need to have an agreement with a surveyor or architect to visit and assess a potential purchase at fairly short notice, and some idea of how funds for a deposit could be secured at equally short notice.

Groups may wish to issue a general announcement or advertisement that they are looking for a site, or for some existing property.

An announcement could be compiled along the lines of:

"…A Cohousing project is keen to find land on which to create a Cohousing scheme of 15-30 self-contained properties plus additional community facilities – or suitable existing property. It is intended that the properties will be for a combination of sale and rent. The project will be especially keen to discuss this proposal with… Please contact:… "

and then sent to the offices of local estate agents, known land agents and even the local press as a formal announcement.

Groups may need to introduce their intentions to a wide range of potential supporters, however there is merit in a focused approach that is designed to influence key perceptions.

We found that making quite a polite but public fuss about the lack of opportunities for alternative housing options to tackle the local housing crisis played out well for us in the press… We believe (at the risk of having delusions of grandeur) that our campaigning brought about a shift in how the council sees housing solutions… Coming to the council with a well thought out solution rather than just asking for land, really helped get support…
[Project in development]

KEY MESSAGE
Groups must be prepared to be pro-active in order to create contact with potential land or property-owners

Identifying land or property

It will be important for groups to be imaginative about the various options of sites or property suitable for a Cohousing project. Not all sites that could be suitable present themselves as typical building plots.

Cohousing Groups would clearly welcome the chance to hear of potential sites or buildings before they are announced on the open market, but that does require establishing good contacts with those who are well connected with the local property scene. There will always be a need for the Group to be actively visiting different parts of their local area to see what opportunities might be coming up.

Such opportunities could be:

Greenfield – land that has not been used for building purposes before, being either pristine fields, a paddock or similar, or land that falls within one of more existing property/ies, such as an acre of a large garden (sometimes such space may also be called 'backland').

Brownfield – a site which used to have a property on it, or which has an unused or derelict property, or which was used in some other way, and that could be suitable for a new purpose, including residential use.

Urban 'renewal' or 'regeneration' sites – land, property or areas that the local authority considers suitable for radical change – either by way of removal and then redevelopment, or through a significant upgrading or remodelling of what exists.

'Section 106' agreements (England & Wales); **'Section 75' agreements** (Scotland); **'Section 76' agreements** (Northern Ireland) – sites with planning approval for residential development and with set obligations about the way the development must proceed (likely in part to require the delivery of land or units for 'affordable housing').

'Rural exception' sites – sites located outside but adjacent to a settlement boundary (invariably a village-sized settlement), for which special planning permission could be sought – almost always to provide affordable dwellings – and for which planning authorities usually have dedicated policies.

Redundant or empty buildings or offices – redundant buildings once used for commercial or manufacturing purposes, or as office accommodation, but that could be remodelled for residential and communal use.

Farm sites and outbuildings – existing farm buildings and associated empty or redundant buildings – especially where there may be a combination of a previous farmhouse and other outbuildings – are particularly suited to 'rural retrofit' proposals, where sites with buildings like barns can be appropriately converted for community use.

We are looking to create a rural retrofit project: buy a property with a large house, barns and cottages. The farmhouse will be the Common House.
[Project in development]

Historic / heritage – some historic buildings may be appropriate for use as the hub or basis for communal purposes and facilities, around which new or remodelled residential accommodation could be created.

Early on we decided to look for old farm properties rather than land. A member noticed the property had come back onto the market and followed it up with the estate agent.
[Project in development]

Consider drawing up a 'site assessment checklist'

The checklist should contain a short summary of the key elements the Cohousing group thinks are most important. This can save real time in helping a group rank and respond to suggestions of potentially suitable land or property, or to quickly dismiss ideas that will not meet the group's agreed specification.

A site assessment checklist could include an initial consideration of:

- overall size (can it provide for the group's ambition?);
- main geographical location;
- main orientation (to compass points);
- access to the site;
- greenfield/brownfield characteristics;
- extent of any existing properties (for potential re-use);
- access to available site utilities;
- proximity to local and community services;
- likely terms of purchase/acquisition.

The idea of using land immediately outside, or on the edge, of an existing village settlement is clearly of interest to some groups wishing to develop Cohousing projects with rural characteristics, and maybe with other land for members to use. In the main, local authority 'exception' site policies may not support the amount or mix of new dwellings that Cohousing projects are seeking.

Planning restrictions prevalent in rural areas (most of our geography) are likely to severely limit potential Cohousing projects due to reaching critical mass at the same time as the need to meet very local housing need in order to gain permission outside of the development envelope.
[CLH-Hub]

This will not be the case for every local authority – the Bridport Cohousing group (www.bridportcohousing.org.uk) obtained approval from Dorset Council for a project of a significant size on the edge of the settlement, and Forgebank (www.lancastercohousing.org.uk) was able to justify use of a site from a failed developer for its own edge-of-village approval.

It is inevitable that some potential sites being considered for a possible Cohousing project will not suit all members of the group. Some may not match the personal aims that individual members may have; some locations may simply be in a part of the area (or country) which does not seem attractive to all.

At the completion of building the Marmalade Lane dwellings, 75% had already been sold to members at discounted prices as a result of the group's own marketing activity and reflected the city's international make-up
[Established community]

It is worth recognising that just as some site choices made by a Cohousing group may turn people away from their project, the prospect of there being a real place that can be an identified and focused site will act as a definite attraction to bring others to the group at a future point.

Keep the planners sweet. Do lots of networking with neighbours and Councillors
[Established community]

KEY MESSAGE

Not all sites will offer opportunities to provide everything that a group might originally want it to do. Be prepared to compromise on what is available before an indeterminate wait becomes damaging to the group's existence.

Site
Build
Live
Design
Finance

Getting the basics right

Cohousing projects have been developed to meet the aspirations of members to live as a group of neighbourly households. The following characteristics, when taken together, will distinguish these projects from other collaborative housing or neighbourhood initiatives:

● the design of the physical form and layout of neighbourhoods maximise contact between residents;

● accommodation is self-contained with significant common facilities and spaces, of which a 'Common House' is a crucial setting for communal activities;

● the scheme is of sufficient size and scale to underpin the desired interpersonal dynamics in that neighbourhood;

● the Cohousing group manages and is responsible for the co-design, co-development and co-organisation of the shared neighbourhood.

Some projects are deliberately intended to be inter-generational, seeking to harmonise a mix of household sizes and ages within one setting. (Springhill - www.springhillcohousing.com)

Other projects are focused upon a collection of households with a common identity – such as some projects, established by older households, for example from age 50 upwards. (Cannock Mill - cannockmillcohousingcolchester.co.uk)

A few projects are focused on a particular 'community of interest', such as projects being developed for occupation by a single gender (to date, this has principally been for women). (New Ground - www.owch.org.uk)

Other projects focus on housing that is mutually affordable to its founding members and to other members in the future.

See the DESIGN section of this Guide for further details and the manner in which potential sites can be assessed in terms of:

● space for sufficient number of residential units;

● indicative placement of the Common House and facilities;

● means of vehicle and pedestrian access;

● other potential common and shared space;

● scope for associated land use (like allotments);

● site orientation;

● environmental impact,

● scope to demonstrate low-impact and climate-friendly elements.

The DESIGN section also contains pointers on engaging an architect with the necessary experience and awareness of Cohousing's needs.

We appointed an architect with lots of experience in Cohousing who understood the design principles... [Few] have this experience and some general guidance on those principles, and guidance on appointing suitable architects, would be welcome.
[Project in development]

"If you do not get the design right you may end up just with a traditional scheme with limited opportunities to socialise! Schemes need to be designed with social integration at its [sic] heart.
[Project in development]

Essential characteristics

The key characteristics described opposite represent the essential 'design' of Cohousing as both a physical and spatial use of a place and its buildings, and a social set of intentions. Cohousing combines both elements of design in a typically innovative manner. McCamant and Durrett, the best-known writers on Cohousing, say:

> *"Whilst some of these characteristics are evident in other forms of collaborative housing schemes, what has made Cohousing distinct from other approaches in practice is how its intentional shared and 'participatory process' maximises the creation of a shared identity and a supportive neighbourhood life... none of these characteristics is unique [to Cohousing], but the consistent combination of all four is."*

LILAC

The manner in which Cohousing projects have incorporated these key characteristics into their neighbourhood forms can be expressed in a variety of completed projects. The distinctive Cohousing design always remains.

The way in which Cohousing neighbourhoods revolve around the weaving of inter-personal and social dynamics between members is crucial to their success. It is clear from experience detailed in the Cohousing literature over the years that such relationships function at their most socially dynamic when

projects are neither too small for members to find a comfortable distance from any local friction that might arise, nor comprised of too many households for members to know one another properly.

To use McCamant and Durrett again (whose experience as architects and project managers comes from working with more than 50 completed projects), *"A Cohousing community that contains 20 to 50 adults seems an optimum size... [but] never more than 50 adults".*

KEY MESSAGE
The social and interactive core that is at the heart of Cohousing places is not arrived at accidentally – it is a combination of clear intent and astute design

Using a Project Manager

A professional may be better at dealing with other professionals

A project manager is someone who will oversee the organisation and implementation of the Cohousing project working with different professionals and regulatory bodies.

This role within property development projects is usually undertaken by construction companies, or by contractors. The project manager is responsible for seeing that all steps of the development project, from inception through to the completion of building and the handover of the properties are completed to time, on budget and to a satisfactory standard.

To hire or not to hire your own project manager

Any contractors or builders engaged in the work may well bring a project manager, but there may be a clear benefit in the Cohousing group engaging its own project manager to act as its key agent to ensure that the special requirements of a Cohousing group are taken fully into account.

This would mean the group employing its own professional who reports to the group (or to a sub-group with delegated authority by the whole group). The project manager can be tasked to drive the development programme (whether at the stage of securing approvals, engaging other professionals, or liaising with funders) and act on behalf of the group to challenge other partners and service providers to deliver outcomes in line with the Cohousing project's interests and timetable.

Understanding the Intricacies

In part, the role of an experienced project manager will be to help the Cohousing group fully understand the intricacies of the different tasks and requirements of the project's development, and the decisions that the group will need to consider at various times and stages of the work. More than this, however, a good project manager will be a prime advocate for ensuring the essential nature and interests of the Cohousing project are fully understood (and in time supported) by all the project's partners and other agents.

It would be great for the network to access a list of architects/project managers with specific experience and expertise in Cohousing. We could then draw on them when a scheme is progressing

[CLH-Hub]

Thundercliffe Grange, Yorkshire

Who pays a project manager?

It is possible that a group might be offered the use of a project manager from a key partner – such as a housing association, or a land-owning developer. In such circumstances a group should be aware that the cost of such an agent will be added to the costs of the project, and this may not be an expense they can control in great detail.

It should also be recognised that agents are, in general, bound to act in accordance with the directions given to them by whoever is immediately paying for their services.

A project manager engaged by an external body to support a Cohousing group may not feel able to advocate on its behalf as forcefully as the group may wish, especially if it involves a challenge to actions undertaken by the partner paying for the manager's services.

Directly employing a project manager may come at a price – but it can clearly help the group's confidence that the project's outcomes will be promoted as it would wish.

Lancaster Cohousing engaged a Project manager separate to the scheme architect

Cannock Mill Cohousing's architect also acted as the manager of the whole development

Can a member of the Cohousing Group undertake the role of project manager?

There will be different views on this, depending on the skills and confidence of individual groups. Using one or more group members to co-ordinate all the issues between other professionals and partners could save on expense but could be a source of tension in the relationship between those members and the rest of the group.

Can the scheme architect also act as the project manager?

Similarly, whilst many architects are used to acting as a project manager for property development schemes elsewhere, the different issues of coordinating the delivery of a range of services for in effect a host of client households may be easier if undertaken by someone who is not also engaged with the implementation of the design and planning detail.

What stage to employ a project manager?

It is never too early for a group to consider engaging its own project manager, who can act as its most prominent active agent in negotiations and meetings with other partners at times when members of the group are busy elsewhere.

Such a manager could be identified or located through the local CLH-Hub, or it could be a service that the Hub is able to offer itself (for an agreed fee).

KEY MESSAGE

The appointment of a group's own project manager to facilitate and inform the development of key partnerships and appointments can also be an invaluable advocate of the project's vision.

Be aware of key factors that will impact on a series of financial decisions

Initial estimates of the costs of a Cohousing project will be similar to other forms of housing or property development. The key factors that will determine these initial costs are:

- The site value – this will be determined by the planning policy requirements for the land or property the group has under consideration and by the condition of the land in its existing use. The local authority planning and housing policies will state the number, type and dwellings and tenures wanted from a site. A survey of site conditions will assess what infrastructure is needed to open up the site. With this information, a valuer can give an idea of the market value of the site.

- The number of dwellings and other property uses that could be located on the site (or from the existing buildings). What can the site or property provide that will suit the scale and range of dwellings that will support the Cohousing vision?

- What might be the most appropriate way of providing for a 'Common House' ? This could be a new building, or a remodelling of existing space and property, such as the ground floor of a multi-storey property.

- What other uses of space may be desired within the new Cohousing neighbourhood? Land required as space for play areas, landscaping or common garden areas will have an impact on the number and density of the residential dwellings.

- Construction costs – a general sense of construction costs in the locality (usually given as £/m^2) can be obtained through information widely available on the internet, and from your architect.

> Further discussion on the potential sources of finance for acquisition and construction costs is detailed in the FINANCE section.

Dôl-Llys Hall

Advice to groups

What price?

Groups may obviously wish to acquire land or property at the least expensive rates, but assumptions by members that a Cohousing project should automatically be able to acquire this at some 'discounted' rate are unlikely to be shared by all other parties unless there is a clear local authority policy to that effect.

A proposed project may be able to obtain a preferential price for a site if it intends to provide outcomes that meet a wide range of local authority policies, but such a position is something for negotiation. It is more likely that starting discussion on a site price and value will have to be based on the core planning policy for a site to deliver the required residential outcomes.

Advice on acquiring sites from the charity sector at prices that reflect the future community-focus of a Cohousing project could review information like :

https://www.gov.uk/government/publications/selling-or-leasing-charity-land-for-less-than-best-price/selling-or-leasing-charity-land-for-less-than-best-price

Groups need to relate key financial decisions – such as the terms under which property could be acquired – back to their overall agreed process of formal decision-making, so that all members can feel mutually engaged with the final outcome.

At the earliest opportunity, initial estimations of costs should be included within material used to attract partners and households to the project.

Produce a business plan with costing of units; produce a brochure identifying what individual property people can get for how much money…
[Established community]

Equally a scheme acquired for a community-led project like a Cohousing one, on the basis of being ready to pay a price that meets the planning policy outcomes for a range of tenures and dwellings, should not be viewed as some kind of 'discounted' scheme. Schemes that will provide policy-compliant outcomes do not in themselves result in land being discounted or reduced in value – the basic value of land is what policy requires from it.

KEY MESSAGES
The finances involved in creating an holistic Cohousing setting should be seen as a whole, in order that the entire shared vision is supported and there is no artificial separation of private and communal space or cost.

Options for acquiring a site

The formal role of a Heads of Terms document will be to set out some initial terms under which a Cohousing group can agree to acquire a site or an existing property, outlining the conditions that have been agreed between the group and the property/site owner. Such initial agreements (sometimes called a 'Memorandum of Understanding') provide a clear indication of the intent by two or more parties to transact together.

In practice, this could be for the transfer or sale of an asset (like land), or for certain services being provided by one party to another (such as an organisation providing a Cohousing group with a range of property development services).

Groups will benefit from having a firm contract stating the agreed basis for determining final purchase values (either for the site or for completed dwellings) to prevent unexpected hikes in costs at a later date.

See detailed information from the CLH website. (www.communityledhomes.org.uk)

The basic options for a Cohousing group to finally acquire a site or other property will include:

- purchase outright on a freehold basis, at market sale prices on the property market – such as Cannock Mill;

- acquire on a long leasehold, e.g. through land that can be provided by a supportive partner, like an umbrella body from the CLH sector, such as Lowfield Green's site from YorSpace in Yorkshire;

- acquire through a joint partnership arrangement between a group and a supportive and active partner, such as Bridport Cohousing's scheme with its local housing association;

- agree a binding 'option' agreement to acquire a site in the future, subject to the satisfaction of certain conditions like the achievement of a completed planning approval on the site, but make sure that any formal option is in the group's own name, and not in the name of another organisation which could decide other uses for the site or simply not proceed with the option to acquire it;

- acquire land that could already be the subject of a prior planning agreement or set of planning conditions from a previous planning approval (such as conditions that will be lodged by planning authorities on large areas of land to be built upon at future dates; note that the conditions are likely to be in different phases or agreements). A Cohousing group could negotiate to acquire a site to meet some of these planning obligations that have been set for the whole area – as was done at Marmalade Lane in Cambridgeshire.

The acquisition of a site will not mean an automatic end to planning uncertainties because there will still be detailed requirements to finalise for planning and building control purposes.

Although we have a site (and some of us live on it) in an existing shared (farm-)house, we are still dealing with early issues related to the (National Park) planning system, and are not yet living this way
[Project in development]

The acquisition of a site (or a clear option for this), is however a major step forward, and groups should also remember to take the time to celebrate such progress!

Formats of legal agreements

Groups may wish to use a 'Heads of Terms' format to record their initial understanding with the land- or property-owner, or they may use a 'Memorandum of Understanding'. At this stage in the project, either format can be used to make the agreement between the group and the site owner more transparent, subject to the stated conditions being met in due course.

Such agreements can also be used to record the manner in which external partners may be engaged by the Cohousing group, and the obligations of the group and the partners to each other. They are likely to state the broad agreement for the properties and tenures that the group wishes to create, and the manner in which the property is to satisfy fundamental Cohousing aspirations.

We are working with our housing association partners on this phase, and although we have not yet secured a site have selected architects and started looking at layouts
[Project in development]

Initial agreements like these will not ordinarily represent formal contracts that spell out the price and conditions under which the sale and transfer of property or land is actually to take place. They are non-binding agreements about the terms under which a group is planning to work with its partners.

[We] will have a housing association partner to own the head leasehold of the affordable housing. We have had discussions about how to take on some [management and maintenance] responsibilities as a group, on a voluntary basis, and those which we may contract to the housing association... [We] have assessed how we want to manage this stage, and decided that we will only work through an enabling development partner structure...
[Project in development]

There is strong interest within the community-led housing sector in more schemes being developed in the future with support and resources that are already held by larger housebuilders and property developers, who are so active (and usually dominant) in the UK's property markets.

Cohousing groups could certainly consider how their ideas for a new Cohousing neighbourhood could fit into wider plans for new housing developments that already have some initial planning approval, particularly if a group's readiness to provide a mix of tenures within their scheme (to include affordable housing tenures) could be a means of showing a developer how the group can help meet pre-set planning obligations. An arrangement between the group and a partner with land might furthermore be considered on the basis of the group procuring other services from the partner. Where sites or properties could be acquired under a form of 'option' agreement, groups will need to clarify whether it is the group or a partner that holds the actual option.

KEY MESSAGE
Groups need to plan for schemes that can create the interpersonal dynamics evident in Cohousing areas elsewhere. On a new site this could be between one and two acres, depending on the number of members and the group's intentions.

CLH Facilitators and Hubs could support projects in the site stage in a number of ways:

Briefs to identify potential sites

Helping groups compile short briefs on their ambitions to identify or locate a suitable site.

*Our hub is made up of local authority officers,
we can explain the process of acquiring
council owned land and buildings*
[CLH-Hub]

Housing policy requirements

Supporting groups to develop proposals that will be compliant with the demands of local housing policy and with the delivery of affordable outcomes within holistic neighbourhoods.

Social value

Helping groups compile social value presentations in support of Cohousing propositions and advocating for local authority policy to release land specifically for 'community-led' projects with strong 'social value' characteristics.

Site design and feasibility

Advocating for local authority policies that can embrace Cohousing designs – site uses; common buildings; mix of tenures; parking preferences; management of affordable housing units – and assisting groups by undertaking initial site feasibility studies and initial financial modelling exercises.

Property acquisitions

Signposting groups to suitable templates for Heads of Terms agreements for sites and for potential works with future partners.

Project managers

Assisting groups with their considerations on appointing a project manager, and undertaking this role if approached.

Key stakeholders (for example local government authorities; second-tier town, parish and community councils; housing associations; developers; etc.) could support projects in the SITE stage through:

Public sector property disposals

Local authorities could adopt asset disposal policies that direct the use of land or redundant buildings to Cohousing and other CLH schemes (www.communityledhomes. org.uk), including possible support for purchase payment of that land to be agreed under deferred arrangements.

Design codes

Understanding of and support for the size and scale of Cohousing settings is crucial, as is support for the overall vision of how sites and buildings are to be used. Enabling the use of flexible design codes to support Cohousing's common facilities, its land uses and its approach to parking provision, will be essential.

It will be helpful for planning authorities to confirm that the 'Common House' and similar shared facilities are accepted as extensions of domestic space and that no separate class of use is considered necessary
[Project in development]

Exception sites

Local 'exception site' policies could be considered more holistically where Cohousing schemes can provide a range of benefits to the wider adjacent community, especially where there is evident support for a Cohousing use of available land.

The difficulty residents have had in trying to get their age-appropriate homes through planning is an example of the difficulties faced by communities of interest in getting schemes through planning.
[CLH Hub]

Neighbourhood Plans

Local planning policies that encourage the development of very local and neighbourhood-specific plans could certainly promote opportunities for Cohousing and other CLH projects.

Wider planning policy

If larger sites are available for residential development planning authorities could demonstrate their support for more than one Cohousing project being developed.

New Ground, North London

Developing the plan

The planning stage of the project involves working with a range of professionals to design the scheme, obtaining planning permission where required and finding the funds to make it happen.

Information on these points is contained in the Finance section

Plan
Build
Live
Design
Finance

A Cohousing scheme, like any other property development project is, at a significant level, a business proposition. It will need to be a convincing proposition both for the ongoing confidence of the group's members, and to create confidence in the project's viability among potential partners. A business plan will enable the group to demonstrate the strength of the proposition and will explain to potential funders or lenders how their funds will be used and how reliable repayments will be.

At some point before a scheme is promoted to any funders or partners, a formal business plan should be prepared to show all its budgets and cash forecasts, and anticipated results. It might be that all its elements only finally come together over a period of time – that will depend on how much information is already available.

At its heart, the business plan will eventually include estimates of:

● all anticipated costs and expenditure used on the project, from inception to completion and immediate occupation (with the potential removal of costs that do not need to be redeemed on scheme completion);

● all anticipated costs of outstanding loan repayments;

● all anticipated income and receipts from the households (and possible other partners) taking up occupation of the completed properties, including rental receipts from any rental properties;

● the anticipated operating costs of the completed neighbourhood's mutual and shared facilities;

● the anticipated income received to cover the operation and management of the mutual and shared facilities, such as from members' future agreements on 'service charges';

● the extent to which payments are received from all households to meet the obligations of the neighbourhood's freeholder (which will in most instances be the Cohousing group), such as for future housing management and maintenance responsibilities;

● the potential key risks to the project's timetable and to its final delivery, set out in a 'risk register';

● groups could consider the scope for negotiating any discount in costs and values that could stem from a larger number of units (say 20+) all being procured from a single external body or partner.

The business plan will furthermore estimate how its costs will be covered by different kinds of finances and funds – whether that is via capital from its members, loans and grants from public or private sources, or revenues (rents and mortgage payments) that the completed scheme brings in over time.

It might also suggest where other sources of funds could be obtained – see the FINANCE section of this Guide.

The robustness of the business plan will be fundamental in getting backing from banks, building societies, funding agencies such as Homes England and other foundations, and from potential partners.

If there [was] a sound business plan I could find a site for a Cohousing scheme in a larger development

A business plan changes and evolves

In the early days of a Cohousing project, the first version of a business plan may be little more than an initial 'statement of financial intent' – it will change and evolve as the details of the scheme begin to be firmed up through input from development finance experts, architects, and land and property valuers.

The plan also becomes the means to demonstrate to existing and future members what participation in the project should mean for each household.

A Cohousing business plan that has been competently constructed and well-presented will enhance a Cohousing group's reputation and strengthen the likelihood of the group meeting its objectives. A plan that is poorly constructed, however, will be easily damaging to the group's reputation, particularly in the view of those stakeholders who have the scope or position to influence the group's future.

A business plan that looks some years into the future will be essential for any application by a Cohousing group which is thinking of applying to the Registrar of Social Housing to become a registered provider (RP) in its own right.

Whilst Cohousing groups need not be intimidated by the prospect of creating a credible and appropriate business plan, there are definite areas that it should present:

- how the project's momentum can be summarised to date;
- how all the pre-development tasks (i.e. the plan stage) will be undertaken;
- how all construction works (i.e. the build stage) will be funded and completed;
- how all the properties and facilities will be used and occupied on completion of the build stage;
- how the future neighbourhood community will undertake its oversight and management of the facilities and properties into the future.

Threshold Centre

Spot the weaknesses before – not after

It is not uncommon for business plans to include costs and revenues for the proposed scheme but lack sufficient detail about how the scheme is to be achieved. Any such lack of detail in explaining how the project's strategy is to be implemented (and its potential costs) will represent a fundamental weakness and create a major barrier to a group's ambitions finding support.

Some of the common weaknesses in business plans include:

- the presentation of the plan appears false, as it is either too scruffy or too slick;

- the length of the text is too long and is full of generalisations;

- the text is too short and too vague;

- there are insufficient facts and details about what is being proposed;

- there are factual errors in the text;

- there are clear omissions in the presentation that suggest necessary skills or resources are lacking;

- there is insufficient consideration or analysis of 'what if...?' situations (e.g. 'what if costs are underestimated?'; 'what if interest rates rise?');

- the overall financial projections are unreasonably optimistic;

- the plan appears more designed to raise finance than to organise the actual delivery of the project;

- the plan was obviously produced by professional consultants, raising doubt about the capability of a project's own management skills.

Canon Frome, Herefordshire

There are some key elements that must be in a Business Plan in order for it to adequately portray the intentions of a Cohousing project.

Some of these elements should be considered 'crucial' to the content of a Business Plan.

Supplementary information can assist in filling out the Cohousing picture but will be less essential for some of the intended audience and potential partners.

Elements 'crucial' for a Cohousing business plan

- vision and objectives of the overall Cohousing project;
- executive summary of the business plan;
- governance structure of the Cohousing organisation (legal format etc.);
- general background detail of people for whom the Cohousing project will provide homes;
- analysis of demand for and interest in Cohousing in the area;
- summary of property and facilities in the proposed Cohousing neighbourhood;
- intended process to implement the Cohousing project and projected timetable;
- project investment plan and asset management of Cohousing neighbourhood;

- statutory, financial and other obligations, and performance targets for the completed project;
- performance monitoring and operational management of the future neighbourhood;
- financial and budgetary forecasts, and income projections;
- details of loan and borrowing strategies of members and any purchase receipts from partners;
- statement on the relationship of the Cohousing project to the wider environment/climate change;
- risk assessments;
- contingency plans.

Elements 'desirable' within a Cohousing business plan

- brief statement from the Cohousing organisation;
- history of the Cohousing project;
- operational infrastructure – how the Cohousing organisation conducts its business; role of sub-groups, etc.;
- peer comparisons with other 'community-based' residential projects;
- other internal aspects of the Cohousing organisation's operations (IT, HR, etc.).

Finance Design Live Build Plan

Each Cohousing project will need to make a judgment about whether to embark on a partnership with a housing developer or a housing association, or to organise the development of the whole project itself, independently of significant assistance from others.

A number of the UK's recent Cohousing projects have been established by groups acting, in effect, as independent developers in their own right, and arranging all the aspects of site acquisition, planning and regulatory approvals, and the management of contractors and their construction work. Such interest will still materialise in some future projects, especially where decisions may be based upon private resources to fund the largest part of the project. Some contemporary groups are now looking at ways to enter into suitable partnerships with housing associations or niche housebuilders and developers who are able to help fund all or some of the costs for the project's development and reduce some of the direct risks to the Cohousing group itself.

It is certainly the case that there is an increasing number of housing associations and smaller developers interested in being a partner with a Cohousing project as a way of participating in socially useful development and at the same time securing some new homes or income for itself.

We linked up with a small housing association who were in those days enthusiastic about building communities

(Established community)

The potential advantages of a Cohousing project having an external partner could include:

- the partner's development expertise and technical advice;

- its ability to find sites or suitable buildings;

- resources to fund the development phase;

- reduced risk for the members of the group;

- the partner's familiarity with achieving planning consents;

- the partner being a body required for the provision of affordable housing units;

On the other hand, coming together with such partners could mean:

- the Cohousing group has less control over the design and development process;

- the group is required to provide guaranteed fees or a percentage of financial return, regardless of other costs;

- the allocation of future properties could need additional agreement outside of the Cohousing group.

The most important requirement for going into partnership is finding a partner that shares the group's vision and that can buy into the philosophy and values of the group's ambitions, avoiding complications in how the final neighbourhood is completed. Without the Cohousing values being fully accepted, there could easily be difficulties related to the way the project is completed and the way the finished neighbourhood is managed. Preliminary agreements (like 'Heads of Terms') should set out the aims of the Cohousing project, the agreed roles of each partner, the size and dimensions of the project to be built, the anticipated costs, fees and timescales for completion of all works, and the way that any future disputes should be resolved. Subsequent formal agreements can shape responsibilities for how the project is to be developed, but this will not mean all uncertainties will be smoothed away.

Local authorities may want an enabling developer but having an enabling developer will not make all problems go away

(Private Sector Developer)

The detail of the Cohousing project's core business plan will include a fundamental decision on whether or not it is intended to find one or more external partners to help the project progress.

The prospect of being able to acquire and rely on an experienced and resourceful organisation, one which could carry out the key tasks that the project will require and maybe also contribute other resources and skills to make it all happen, is bound to seem an attractive one – especially if this could happen early into the life of the project.

Several housing associations will probably work with Cohousing
[CLH-Hub]

A methodical way for the group to approach this matter (and not to rush into hasty agreements with bodies of which they have no prior knowledge) is to draw up a clear summary of what kind of support and services are wanted, and to use this as a way to discuss matters with potential partners.

Who decides what gets provided?

The very act of taking a methodical and serious approach to finding a partner for a project's progress should itself be viewed positively by external interests. It will enhance the credibility of the Cohousing project and make it more likely to be seen as a well-balanced endeavour which would be attractive to potential partners.

Each group needs to be clear in its own mind of its particular reasons and rationale for finding an external partner.

We needed to talk to Housing Associations about how to recruit to the affordable housing element
[Co-op in development]

KEY MESSAGE

It is vital that a group's partner understand their Cohousing values from project inception through to completion and occupation

Even if a group had only one external body with whom they might consider a future partnership, the following points or questions should be explored with them::

1. What is their understanding of the term 'Cohousing'?

2. Have they any previous experience of working with a 'Cohousing' project or a community-led housing group?

3. How would they respond to the group being the key commissioners? What else would they suggest?

4. What resources could they bring to the planned project – land? property? access to lenders? grant?

5. What decisions would be taken by each partner and what would be shared?

6. How would they involve the group in decisions on overall design and financial solutions?

7. How familiar are they with responding to local authority policies, and with procedures for grant-aided works?

8. Which employees would work on this project and would they be available in the evenings or at weekends?

9. What would be the cost of their participation? What financial return would they want?

As professional property development projects, Cohousing schemes will be required to use an architect or designer who is appropriately experienced in working with collective community housing projects. Even if the formal appointment is undertaken through a group's partner (such as a housing association) groups need to be clear which design skills need to be available for their project.

We need a list of architects that work on Cohousing

The following methods could identify suitable design professionals:

● run an open recruitment process via a public invitation or design competition;

● ask for recommendations from other community-led projects or supporters of the group;

● ask an external partner whether they already have a contractual arrangement with a suitable supplier of design skills (such as architects already used by a housing association or housing developer);

● look within the group for any members with suitable design skills and experience (as at Cannock Mill). [Groups will need to reflect on the overall role a scheme architect must undertake and examine whether a formal engagement of a member to this role may introduce undue strain into other relationships within the project.]

There is a mass of supplementary information on Cohousing design that Groups should discuss with their chosen agent(s,) in order to make use of existing guidance and the experience of completed projects elsewhere.

Some Cohousing projects have admitted having a lack of awareness about existing sources of information and advice on Cohousing design matters. Architects and designers offering their services could be questioned on their understanding of key points from sources noted in the RESOURCES section of this Guide.

This is a process of learning for yourselves as a group what works for you, what you like and what you want

Design drawings routinely go through several iterations, so the Cohousing group will need to make clear to their architects that they will be required to maintain the ongoing involvement and considerations of the group's members, in other words, to recognise that it is ultimately the group's members who are the final clients who will be living on the site and in the dwellings created.

Professionals will need to be sensitive to suggestions about how the principles of Cohousing design are applied in practice, especially concerning the functions and design of the project's Common House and shared facilities.

A Cohousing group's project manager could have a central role in coordinating the group's responses to design ideas and would be likely to spend a lot of initial time liaising with the architectural team. Even where a project's partners like a housing association or private developer may have a major role in how the scheme might progress, they are likely to accept the architect as the main mediator of a 'co-designed' process, so the choice of architect and the means of the liaison with the group will always need to be made carefully.

The ultimate use by a Cohousing project of suitable design skills is a crucially important matter which a group needs to be confident about. The group must feel it will have an appropriate professional and balanced working relationship with the chosen designer or architect.

We appointed an architect with lots of experience of Cohousing who understands the design principles

[Project in development]

Finding such a suitably experienced designer or architect could be achieved through a group inviting potential agents to return an 'expression of interest' that would be the first stage in being 'interviewed' for such an appointment. The next stage would then be a more formal interview, undertaken by the group, at which an agent's credentials and experience could be examined in more detail.

Questions to ask a designer/architect in an interview (even where a group has only one to meet or interview):

1. What is their understanding of the term 'Cohousing'?

2. Have they visited a Cohousing neighbourhood? [If yes, ask for details]

3. Have they any experience of working with, or being part of, a Cohousing or other community group? [If yes, ask for details]

4. How have they involved/would they involve a group in decisions on final residential design ideas?

5. Have they any experience of working with mixed-income initiatives? [If yes, ask for details]

6. Who from the agent's office would be involved in this project, if appointed, and what is their experience?

7. Will they be available for meetings at evenings or weekends, if required?

8. What is the architect's experience of work within a wider project, where another agent may oversee their input? [Ask for details]

9. What would be the basis of their fees, and when would payment(s) be required?

The formal process of appointment should set clear parameters for how the relationship is to be a business relationship and undertaken in that way. The promotion of the Cohousing ideal can be intoxicating even for engaged professionals, but a group will want to feel confident that key decisions and evaluations will still be brought back to the collective body for sufficient consideration, and not commandeered by professional interests.

KEY MESSAGE

Both the scheme architects and the project's members need a firm understanding of Cohousing design. Groups could use this Guide's 'Basic Principles of Cohousing Design' as a discussion and awareness-raising tool.

Some of these professions may be needed for a short while, such as to secure planning permissions or provide initial advice on construction costs, and may not need to be thoroughly quizzed on their understanding of, or support for, the core principles of the Cohousing ambitions. It would be necessary, however, for the group – perhaps again through its tasks given to the project manager – to ensure the professionals being used are fully knowledgeable about the neighbourhood environment that is being sought through the co-design and collaboration of the project's members, especially the end result of the core designs professionals

Finding the right agents

The search and appointment process noted above will also apply to any appointment of other professionals that could be required for contributory elements of a Cohousing project:

- quantity surveyors (for all elements of assessing financial costs and calculations);

- building surveyors or engineers to check construction methods or assess properties;

- employer's agent and/or clerk of works (for roles in the construction process);

- legal advisors (for conveyancing and contractual matters);

- other financial advisors (for consideration of funding sources and obligations);

- interior designers (if advice is wanted on the interior and materials in the Common House);

- landscape designers (for potential advice on external areas and common gardens);

- planning consultants (if advice is required to gain planning permission).

East Whins

The website of Community Led Homes website provides a number of templates for engaging professional agents that Cohousing projects could use for their appointments. (www.communityledhomes.org.uk)

Members of the group need to be closely involved in deciding what is written into such agreements, but it is likely to be its own key agent like a project manager who will be central in helping members choose who to appoint and why.

The project managers used by projects such as Forgebank and Springhill and LILAC were key to orchestrating the variety of short-term or longer relationships that their projects had with different professional services, acting as a daily link between the group and those advisors and helping to translate issues that naturally arose for all parties to digest and address.

Where a Cohousing project has agreed to use a key partner to manage progress of the detailed design and construction, then the engagement of the professionals could well take place through that partner's customary arrangements; **it will be sensible for a group to ascertain the implications that such standing arrangements could have for them as the 'client'.**

KEY MESSAGE

Whether the engagement of professional advice to the Cohousing project is undertaken directly by a group, or by an agreed partner, members need to retain a core role in the appointment process used.

Don't reinvent the wheel

The design material included in this Guide is to help members provide clear instructions to their architects or designers for what is wanted from the project's identified site.

The 'Basic Principles of Cohousing Design' (produced with this Guide) can be a tool for introducing crucial elements of the way Cohousing settings can be shaped, both in presenting basic concepts to potential partners and for a group to debate principles of co-design by itself.

Feedback on the do's and don'ts of the Common House design and operating costs would be really useful

Other detailed design guides about how to conceive Cohousing projects are available. Those written in English are mainly from North America, such as an informative guide on the design of the Common House. www.issuu.com/schemataworkshop/docs/ cohousing_common_house_design There are few other guides targeted at an introductory level written for a UK audience with UK examples.

[I have] never seen this kind of information about basic design, and with a range of UK examples...

Cohousing projects stand out from other collaborative housing projects because the design process involves both the physical shaping of the physical environment, and the social shaping of the environment to foster the relationships that members want for their subsequent community and neighbourhood life.

This is therefore a combination of the physical layout and juxtaposition of all elements of the neighbourhood's built and natural environments with deliberate attention given to how to establish this communal and shared identity that will sustain the desired relationships.

This can be a crucial feature in how projects introduce themselves to other neighbours around the proposed Cohousing site. The group will be keen that the development is not seen as another 'speculative' housing project, or an inward-looking gated community, dumped on the doorsteps of the surrounding community.

New Ground

86

How will the design be agreed?

How will the group's members agree with their designers that the final designs encapsulate what they want, and could be ready to submit for approval from the local planning authority?

The following self-assessment could help evaluate whether a group feels ready for such a submission:

● Does the proposed layout of the site and the placement of the scheme's major elements (dwellings, common facilities, gardens, parking) feel like it will generate deliberate and incidental contact and interactions between site residents?

● Are the proposed dwellings of the desired sizes and amounts, and does it feel like they will have an appropriate mix of privacy and communality?

● Is the Common House being placed where it can maximise the opportunity to be at the heart of daily activity for all members?

● Will the buildings and facilities be accessible, flexible and adaptable to accommodate changes in household circumstances, personal mobility, etc.?

● How much of the group's original vision is evident in the proposed final designs? If there is now a fair amount of difference from original ideas, are the group's members sufficiently content with the proposed outcome and the reasons for this?

Be circumspect of thinking that 'tiny homes' are a suitable basis for log-term accommodation... There is clearly a time and place for some households (and housing projects) to use versions of 'tiny homes', however small properties will certainly not be sufficient for households needing space for their mobility needs, nor assist long-term occupation and households increasing their sizes. The idea that Cohousing is conducive to smaller properties is practical in places where house sizes are generous, however design approaches common across the UK housing sector have already meant that its dwellings are amongst the smallest in Europe!

There was a two-phase design process... organised into workstreams enabling the Cohousing group to be involved with the professional team as the design was developed after the successful bid.

KEY MESSAGE
How much of the proposed final designs have already been discussed with planners or with elected Councillors from the local authority? Has any of the design received negative responses to date? Groups could consider whether there are some potential 'champions' inside the authority who could help the group address any uncertainties about design matters that might be held by the planning service.

Although the planning systems of the devolved nations have a separate legal basis to the planning system in England, their technical designs are still very close to the existing system in England. They are still highly discretionary, as decisions to grant planning permission are frequently made case-by-case. [A useful overview of the UK's planning systems is UK Parliament Commons Library Briefing Paper 07459 available from commonslibrary.parliament.uk/research-briefings/cbp-7459]

It is essential that groups find out about local planning policies at an early stage to assess how their scheme is likely to be received by the local planning authority and whether there are particular policy measures to be mindful of. This will initially involve looking at adopted local planning documents which contain the planning authority's core and 'supplementary' policies and any relevant special measures that may apply, such as 'rural exception site' policies, conservation areas or other local protection measures in force. It should be noted that National Park authorities control planning within the UK's national park boundaries.

You need to undertake a persuasion phase with the local planners to help them understand the vision: having a project manager helped us to achieve this
[Established community]

It is vital for groups to take time to understand what the Local Plan says about places, sites and buildings across the entire local authority and what additional policies any subsequent Neighbourhood Plan may have approved for a specified village, parish or neighbourhood area. These considerations are particularly relevant for Cohousing schemes that are aimed primarily at households wanting to create new living arrangements together. Such proposals could, of course, be presented as a positive way to meet other policies the local authority has adopted to support sustainable development and innovative local community aspirations.

The challenge is to make the scheme affordable and justify it as an exception to existing planning policy
[Group in development]

Planning applications and permissions

The process of submitting applications for formal approvals contains the following elements and stages:

- 'pre'-application opening discussions with planning officers;

- submission of a planning application in 'outline' or as 'full';

- public consultation over the application;

- local authority assessment of conformance of the proposed scheme to Local Plan policies, and of responses to public consultation;

- decision by council planning committee (or designated officers);

- post-decision completion of all formal and legal agreements stipulating planning requirements;

- final approvals confirmed in full.

An outline planning application will require little design detail but can require drawings and measurements to provide a precise statement of the number, type and tenure of any dwellings, and of other features such as a proposed Common House and edge-of-site parking. The local authority will undertake a customary degree of open public consultation on any planning application but there would be good reason for the Cohousing group to offer additional consultation with the local community to provide reassurance on its plans and garner neighbourhood support.

Full planning application

A full planning application will require detailed drawings and other back-up information on site access, vehicle use and parking, landscaping and open spaces and utilities plus surveys, assessments and statements of broader community involvement. It can also often require a negotiated final agreement on the nature of final planning obligations. Planning applications can be modified within an agreed time, if circumstances change, but a newapplication may be required if the changes are considered substantial, at which point a new fee could be charged.

Legal and planning agreements and 'infrastructure levy' requirements

These frame binding obligations that will be part of the terms of final planning approvals, usually to provide for mitigation measures that are supposed to offset the impact of the new development on the existing environment and local community.

There are ways to meet local authority priorities and satisfy the needs of the community

'Section 106' agreements (England and Wales); **'Section 75'** agreements (Scotland) and **'Section 76'** (Northern Ireland) are a common way for local planning policy requirements to be embedded in final legal agreements. Common requirements in such agreements are for a percentage of the dwellings to be 'affordable housing' and for other contributions to be made to school provisions, or health or policing services. Some of these may add extra costs to a Cohousing scheme; some may not. It is usually a matter for negotiation between the local authority and the applicant (or their agent).

LILAC

Finance Design Live Build Plan

Building Regulations

Any building scheme will also require building regulations consent from the building control section of the local authority. The requirements for buildings and other developments to be constructed in a required and approved manner are not part of planning regulations regulations but are covered by technical regulations set by each national assembly or government, with subtle variations between them. Commencing works without building regulation approval in place could risk those works being ordered to be dismantled or demolished.

It will be a key role for the scheme architect to ensure that the drawings and details prepared for a Cohousing scheme comply with the appropriate regulations. Even where the aspirations of the Cohousing project are for its building standards to be in excess of the minimum requirements, and thereby higher than conventional neighbourhood schemes, it is important that the correct standards are being applied to the whole Cohousing scheme.

When considering the standards, the Common House facilities need to be evaluated as extensions of domestic space (albeit suitable for a large group) but not as space intended for public events as that second designation will have additional standards and requirements. Even where it could seem apparent that such common facilities could be open to others who visit a Cohousing community, care needs to be taken that the Cohousing facilities are viewed as primarily for use by the scheme's residents, rather than being intended for public benefit.

Local Lettings

The planning process is likely to require a firm conclusion to any agreements between the project and the local authority on how 'affordable' units are to be occupied – both for first occupations at the time of the scheme's completion and for subsequent occupations when those dwellings become vacant in the future.

This will be the time for agreement to be confirmed in a clear and public document that those lower-income households who have been active members of the Cohousing group throughout the development period to date will be accepted as eligible to occupy appropriate affordable units.

Projects will also wish to have clarified the agreed parameters for finding future households to occupy these units. They may wish to use versions of other local lettings arrangements or agreements which include criteria that future households should have connections to the scheme by virtue of residency, family or employment as well as a commitment to living in a 'Cohousing' community.

Charges for self-build projects

Each Cohousing group needs to be aware of how the local planners may consider that infrastructure levy rates could apply to their scheme. At present, schemes that are designated as 'self-build' – a definition which most authorities can accept for 'group-commissioned' schemes – are likely to be exempt from rates. Projects may therefore consider whether or not there will be a benefit for them to register their proposals as a 'group self-build' scheme. Groups should check very directly on this matter, but still be realistic about the potential for their scheme to require payment of some charges (and include this in their calculations of different financial scenarios).

Unless the local planning context is fully understood, groups can waste a great deal of time and money.

The planning process is very confusing to new groups

A Cohousing scheme must present its intentions in terms that can appropriately meet statutory policy requirements. Establishing a good relationship with the officers of the local planning department can certainly pay dividends.

Get to know your local planning department and ensure your local authority understands what Cohousing is

Working within the grain of what the local planning system is promoting and making a solid case for the outcomes and benefits of Cohousing can help pave the way for finding successful support. It may also lead to opportunities to make a case for widening how local policy could be interpreted.

Planners should look at schemes more holistically because of the range of wider benefits

To become familiar with the local policy context, groups should investigate the main housing development policies noted in the immediate Local Plan or other authority-wide Planning Frameworks, and look at aspects such as densities of new development, appearance and design, transport access, parking, building height limits, landscape issues, and sustainability measures (such as low carbon energy requirements). What could be contained within the local authority's housing needs assessment as its current priorities? And how could these policies constrain or support what the Cohousing group wants in the final designs and layouts?

Springhill

KEY MESSAGE

Where a Cohousing project wants its proposals to be accepted as a legitimate vehicle for creating a new neighbourhood, it should acknowledge that local requirements could require its outcomes to meet policy levels for economic affordability and inclusivity.

Plan

Build

Live

Design

Finance

CLH Facilitators and Hubs could support projects in the plan stage through:.

Help with business plans

Supporting groups to compile an effective business plan that will set out the risks and assessments of their intended project.

Financial assessments

Undertaking assessments if so commissioned by groups, or being a 'critical friend' in helping groups consider other financial assessments prepared for them.

Assistance with professional appointments

Helping groups consider and appoint suitable agents for professional tasks and providing suggestions for such agents if asked.

Forgebank

Key stakeholders (for example local government authorities; second-tier town, parish and community councils; housing associations; developers; etc.) could support projects in the PLAN stage through:

Local planning frameworks

Some stakeholders may be able to help with including specific mention of Cohousing projects and opportunities in formal documentation and policies for local plans, supplementary planning documents and design codes.

Affordable housing

Specific support could be available for Cohousing projects to help them identify households to occupy the proposed affordable tenancies, at early stages of the projects.

Project management

Public or private sector bodies may consider the seconding an existing employee to be engaged by a Cohousing project as their dedicated project manager.

Laughton Lodge

Marmalade Lane Cohousing, Cambridgeshire

Embarking on the build

Building or renovating the homes is the expensive, risky and fun stage of any project. There is no 'correct' option here – choose whatever suits the project and could best satisfy the planning and building permissions that have been secured.

● Construction options *96*

▦ Securing development finance *154*

● Appointing contractors *100*

● Agreeing the construction programme *102*

● Homes under construction or renovation *104*

 Information on these points is contained in the Finance section

Finance Design Live Build

Construction options – 1

How does it get built?

This is probably the stage in a Cohousing project that is most similar to other building development projects – the organisation and management of the building works to ensure that construction is conducted to meet the planning and design approvals.

Decisions already taken will have determined key construction matters like:

● the scale of the proposed development;

● whether this is for new-build property, for the renovation of an existing property, or for a combination of these;

● what kinds of property are to be constructed for the dwellings and for the community and shared facilities;

● what infrastructure works (e.g. road access, drainage, land reclamation, utilities) are needed.

There are four standard options for bringing forward the actual construction works:

1. The group becomes the direct commissioner of the construction works, thereby taking control of the build process, often using the services of a paid project manager or project management team to represent them in dealing with other professionals and construction-related firms. A smaller project group at Forgebank acted as the key link for the group to commission all the professional advice that their scheme would use. (www.lancastercohousing.org.uk)

2. The group contracts out the management and undertaking of the build works to an external development company which manages all the construction works and delivers the finished properties to the group – like the Marmalade Lane project in Cambridge (www.cambridge-k1.co.uk) or the Threshold Centre (www.thresholdcentre.org.uk) which partnered with a local housing association to navigate through the development and construction process.

3. The group uses the services of a specialist developer via a full 'design and build' arrangement – the developer/builder provides the build designs (to the group's basic specifications) and then undertakes the construction works either on-site or through off-site manufacture of the commissioned units by a factory supplier, building the properties in the factory and then erecting them on-site.

4. The group considers self-build or custom-build options, either for its members to undertake some of the build works directly, or to complete work to properties provided by a contractor (such as an amount of internal finishes and fittings to be completed by the incoming resident households).

A range of case studies is available on the UK Cohousing Network's website, with details of such commissioned works.

Decisions for how a project is to progress with one or other of the above choices will have been taken during tasks undertaken in the plan stage to ensure that all regulatory requirements are already in hand and the project is clear about how the next key activities are to be done.

Where groups are partnering with an external body like a housing association, or a housing developer, key decisions may also have already been taken on how the construction works are to be arranged, in accordance with the partner's usual procedures.

As indicated in the SITE section of this Guide, groups may have decided to appoint an appropriately experienced project manager from outside the group. He or she will assist them in dealing with the detailed and at times complex demands of this stage of Cohousing projects.

> *We would recommend groups work with a construction partner or employ an experienced project managment*
> [CLH-Hub]

How does it get built?

There are a few pros and cons for each of the basic options for how the proposed building works could be undertaken – listed below. They are not mutually exclusive.

Directly commissioning building contractors

The use of a small 'project sub-groups' of members in projects like Forgebank, Lancashire and Springhill, Gloucestershire was certainly exacting and time-consuming for those members involved, and it is crucial that sufficient processes are put in place by the whole Group to enable information and updates to be relayed to the rest of the membership as the construction works proceed

Using a contractor or partner body to organise the works

Having an established external housing body (like a housing association or a housing developer) to co-ordinate and implement the construction works can certainly simplify the demands placed upon Group members – Marmalade Lane in Cambridgeshire used an external development company with established links to a further housing construction firm, and two projects under development in the Manchester area are actively seeking suitable associations or developers.

Design and build

A Cohousing project might consider the use of a 'design-and-build' construction method if it was confident that a tender could be obtained from a contractor that could offer an inclusive, non-negotiable price for the works which represented good value for money. Properties provided through a manufacturing supplier could also be a plausible option to obtain a cost-effective set of works.

Finance   Design   Live   Build

Construction options – 2

Decisions and details

To have satisfactory outcomes from partnerships or professional engagements, the group needs to firmly establish:

- What decisions will remain open to them to influence as the scheme is built out?

- What will they delegate to an external partner?

A key challenge in reaching an agreement on these matters can arise when a partner body has accepted more of the on-site financial risks than the group during the construction period. The partner may then want to exercise more control over the details of the development as it proceeds, and possibly more of the financial rewards. Some groups have found it useful to raise their own awareness of the overall development and construction process by undertaking online training sessions in property development issues, or short courses run by the Chartered Institute of Housing – www.cih.org.

Understanding Construction Documents

Groups will do well to familiarise themselves with what will be required from contractors that could undertake the construction works. It will help to be aware of the role of the different documents and agreements that will shape the formal engagement of such bodies. Two overviews of such documentation can be found at:

- www.countfire.com/blog/different-types-of-construction-contracts

- www.thebalancesmb.com/contract-documents-for-every-construction-project-844919

Construction work at Marmalade Lane

It could be feasible for the Cohousing project to consider taking on a more discrete part of the proposed building works as a 'self-build' engagement that the group could undertake. The Lowfield Green project in York took that approach to evaluating the potential costs of constructing its Common House, both to see if there could be savings in the final construction costs and to see what employment-related training might stem from such works.

Construction work at Forgebank

Self Build – Could we build it ourselves?

Very few recent community-led schemes have used self-build or custom-build methods to build or complete an entire project on the scale of contemporary Cohousing developments. The group-led self-build project at Ashley Vale in Bristol stands out as a vibrant example of a project where individual households mainly took responsibility for their individual plots, echoing historic examples of groups building in common, but without key facilities like a Common House.

Off-site Manufacture

There can be definite advantages of off-site manufacture in terms of potential cost savings, quality control and speed of delivery in the basic construction, but there has not been much take-up of off-site modular housing use by CLH projects to date, not least because such manufacturers usually want a higher number of units to be ordered than many small CLH projects will want. A Cohousing project wanting a larger number of units could consider issuing an 'expression of interest' to a few manufacturers, to gauge what appetite there might be for such a commission.

Build

Live

Finance Design

 KEY MESSAGE
Groups need to understand that the construction stage is a crucial point at which all partners' potential costs and returns become manifest.

Appointing contractors

Understanding the logical sequence

The process of confirming the appointment of contractors or other builders to construct the Cohousing properties usually follows a logical sequence:

● preparing a brief for the detailed construction works;

● organising a tendering process to invite suitably equipped and experienced construction firms to submit a tender for how and when they would propose to undertake all the work required, how they would achieve the required quality of outcomes, and what fees they would require to carry out those works;

● shaping and undertaking a selection process to assess received tenders according to group criteria and weighting and select a candidate with whom to proceed (this process may also involve interview, to obtain further information from prospective appointees and on which a final selection may be based);

● negotiating the contract conditions including timetable for start and completion.

The appointed contractor (or builder) will have its own work practices for organising the works on-site, either by its own operatives or by others engaged on a sub-contract basis. Hopefully, the clarity of the way they conduct those practices is one of the reasons that a Cohousing project has given them the construction contract!

Where a Cohousing project has taken full responsibility for this stage of its project, it will require a clear management process. This may go through the group's project manager or another of the project's agents, such as the scheme architect (many of whom routinely undertake the management of this process).

If a Cohousing group has agreed that the selection and appointment of the construction body will be undertaken by a partner (whether that is a housing association or a private developer), the group should seek to be part of the process in order to ensure that the distinctive quality of the Cohousing scheme is fully understood by whoever is appointed.

Construction at Bridport

Advice to Groups

Groups will always need to check that their constitution and legal structures permit the project to be formally engaged in contractual arrangements with external professional agents.

Finding potential contractors to invite to the tender process will involve compiling suitable names and details from:

● personal suggestions;

● recommendations from architects, developers and other projects;

● advice from local bodies/agent.

The tasks in this stage of the project that groups would give to their project manager would include:

- *assisting with final cost appraisals of the detailed works required in the construction period;*
- *instigating the tendering process and appointment of the builders and contractors;*
- *coordinating the sequential activities of the construction programme with the necessary external agencies and regulatory interests;*
- *overseeing the build works to the timescales, budgets and specifications agreed and liaising between the builder and group in relation to any problems with, or deviations from, the agreed plan;*
- *managing the funds secured for the works in order to meet the cash demands of paying for elements of the work at agreed times.*

Checks and Revisions

Groups need to be engaged with any necessary checks or revisions that may be required to the initial construction costs returned from a contractor. Check all the proposed costs of construction elements. If cost savings are required to bring costs back within the available budget (what some term as 'value engineering') it may be necessary to consider a change of material, or a reduction from the initial quality of the dwellings (maybe PassivHaus construction is less feasible). A check could be made that internal costs per m2 reflect the proposed uses of different buildings. For example, the Common House costs should be slightly lower per m2 than other areas, if this is basically only a communal-sized kitchen and dining space.

KEY MESSAGE

Groups must be rigorous in their oversight of how tendering and appointments are managed – and seek to be an integral part of the formal appointment process, even if this is being co-ordinated by an external partner

Whether you are partnering with a developer or tackling the project as a group development, you'll need a paid project manager or project management team to keep the ten thousand details coordinated
[McCammant and Durrett, 2014:226]

Build

Live

Design

Finance

Agreeing the construction programme

The Group as the ultimate commissioning agency

Construction will be undertaken in accordance with the schedule, costings and specification set out in the contract agreed with the builder or contractor.

The role of a group's own project manager during the construction/build period will be to act as the principal interface between the group and all the external agencies and construction professionals that are engaged in that construction contract. That appointee needs to be experienced in multi-unit housing developments and should have a ready understanding of the aims of the group in order to articulate and communicate any issues to and from the group appropriately.

The work will, however, also be regularly and routinely checked by external inspectors for compliance with:

● the requirements of the project's planning approval (such as treatment of the natural environment and trees or for heights and placements of new buildings);

● building regulations requirements (laying of drains and utilities; wall and insulation materials);

● requirements set within formal planning agreements (such as conditions for the amount and type of affordable housing; or low carbon energy requirements)

In order for a new scheme to be completed as efficiently and cost-effectively as possible, it is important to avoid unnecessary and potentially costly changes during construction.

Group members need to allow contractors to undertake their work (with appropriate oversight by the project manager) and to deliver the work to the schedule, budget, materials and specification set out in the build contract.

It is vital that the details of providing these works on-site are open to final review by the group as the ultimate commissioning agency before the planned works are committed to a final contract.

Construction work at Cannock Mill

Getting the sequence right

It will be important to agree the order and delivery of the dwellings and the other facilities in ways that support ongoing community dynamics.

Unless the community has decided to be practically involved in the construction works to complete the Common House, the delivery of the Common House and other communal facilities needs to take place at the same time as the dwellings so the community's vision is realised as soon as possible. Cohousing projects elsewhere have suffered from taking up residence of their properties without the Common House being ready or useable, and then seeing neighbourhood habits develop without the immediate impetus of the common facilities helping to consolidate community relationships.

Group members could arrange to view the building works at times agreed between the contractor and the project manager but should avoid trying to make detailed examinations of the work unless there are specific concerns that a meeting on-site has been arranged to address. If specific concerns cannot be satisfactorily resolved by the project manager in liaison with the contractors, then the project may need to consult its solicitor or legal advisor in relation to whether or not the terms of the original contract are being kept.

If there is any intention for group members to visit the site and the works during the construction period, insurance should be in place to cover group members being on the site and in the proximity of all materials and building processes.

Don't forget the garden!

A detailed plan for the gardens, landscaping and any exterior work necessary will be an integral element of the overall Cohousing design. This critical aspect of a project can sometimes be underappreciated, leading to further expense and additional preparation work late on in the project, when residents' attention turns to settling-in to their new homes

> *The garden was at the end of the project, and we had no money. We called a meeting to discuss ideas and the atmosphere exploded! It was a really big challenge at the end of a long development process.*
> [Established community]

KEY MESSAGE
Avoid allowing group members to tweak works to 'their property' once construction has started on-site. Changes at this stage can delay the work and creates potential for disputes when final costs are apportioned to the group and to properties.

Finance Design Live Build

Inspection and quality control

The building works taking place will be covered by at least two layers of quality control, possibly three:

- Firstly, the contract will set out a staged schedule, where the project manager (or scheme architect) will check the quality of work and authorise payment to the contractor in accordance with the contracted specification and their professional satisfaction.

- Secondly, statutory building inspections will be required at set stages throughout the build by a registered building inspector (an inspector from the building control department of the local authority or an approved independent inspector).

- Thirdly, insurance warranty inspections will also be required. (An independent inspector would be able to undertake both a warranty inspection and a building regulations inspection that can satisfy the local authority's procedures.)

Other monitoring inspections could also be required for groups using specific loan finance, as required by each lender.

The statutory inspections will identify any major defects with the building that will need to be rectified before the build contract is signed off.

A final round of building and warranty inspections will be undertaken after all internal fixings and decoration have been completed, at which point buildings can be deemed fit for occupation. 'Snagging' inspections are designed to identify any minor faults with the buildings and their fittings (that would not necessarily fail building regulations). The main contractor should undertake its own inspection prior to its presentation of works as 'completed', at which point the project manager or an independent inspector should undertake their own final survey to assess any defects or departures from the required works before the Cohousing project takes possession of the buildings.

A sum of money is usually withheld until any last issues have been adequately resolved by the builder – this could be 5% of the construction contract figure.

Any building defects emerging after the group has taken possession will need to be addressed either by direct negotiation with the builder or under the building warranty.

Quality and satisfaction

It is an unfortunate fact that surveys on the quality of, and satisfaction with, UK building construction works have routinely shown significant frustrations with the end result. The housing charity Shelter found that:

> *"51% of homeowners of recent new builds in England had experienced major problems including issues with construction, unfinished fittings and faults with utilities"*
>
> *[YouGov survey, Guardian, 2 March 2017]*

CAUTION

It is understandable for a group to want the on-site quality control of construction works to be properly monitored and addressed. However, this is not something that can be undertaken by members on any ad hoc basis. The site of the work is still a construction site, governed by health and safety requirements, and is not a place for unauthorised personnel. Members of a group may feel that they can venture onto site to look at 'their' properties, or feel that they can express opinions in being the ones who have commissioned the overall works, but the manner in which works must proceed on-site will not allow such spontaneous visits to the site. Communications and discussion about the works must be conducted though the channels set up for that discussion, and via the personnel put in place for that role – such as a group's project manager.

Construction work at Forgebank

 KEY MESSAGE
Dealing with matters that have come to light through the 'snagging' period can feel like it never has an end. Do not be distressed by this continuing into occupation periods, as this is the time when members need to test the integrity of the buildings that have been delivered to them.

Build

Live

Design

Finance

CLH Facilitators and Hubs could support projects in the build stage through:

Choosing the construction process

Advising groups and supporting them to consider details of how comparable schemes have decided what method of construction works are most suitable..

Tendering and appointment of contractors

Helping groups to put the most appropriate tender process together and participating in the selection process, if requested.

Development finance

Advising on which lenders could be amenable to the Cohousing scheme's ambitions to meet construction costs and on what terms other projects have secured such finance.

On the Brink

Support from Key Stakeholders

Key stakeholders (for example local government authorities; second-tier town, parish and community councils; housing associations; developers; etc.) could support projects in the BUILD stage through:

Regulatory services and visits during on-site phase

They may clear information on the outcome of visits and inspections to the Cohousing group, as well as to the construction body engaged with the works.

Cash flow for construction works

Local authorities or housing association partners may help a project access funds to give them sufficient liquidity in place (cash) to meet payments demanded by phases of the construction programme.

Finance towards affordable tenures

Local authorities or housing association partners may help projects apply for any public grant that could be used for demolition of existing buildings, or any 'abnormal' site preparation expenses.

Peripheral parking at Laughton Lodge

Finance Design Live Build

Laughton Lodge, Sussex

Living in Cohousing Communities

Finally, people can start living in the homes! This is just the start though – managing and maintaining the properties is crucial for the longevity of the project and for household satisfaction. Do this well and the Cohousing project will succeed for decades to come.

 Information on these points is contained in the Finance section

Build

Live

Finance Design

Moving in

When? How? What?

If moving house is one of life's stress points, then moving in to Cohousing can be that experience with knobs on. But this is what you've been waiting for – maybe in some cases for years.

During the construction phase it is good to have something else to think about and focus on. You really need to keep out of the contractors' way and let them get on with it. Use this time to plan your move both as a community and as an individual household.

The few months before anyone moves into your Cohousing project can become quite chaotic. Some members may be in the process of moving into temporary accommodation; others may be tied up with selling their current property; some may live close by while others may be trying to stay in touch from a distance.

A number of things can be done as a community to try and make

the move go smoothly and to support each other in what can be a difficult time. Think through what it will be like to all move at the same time. And remember it is unlikely to be the same experience for everyone – some people will be perpetual movers and take things in their stride; others may have lived in the same home for years and not recall what moving entails.

Remember as a project you may get a staggered handover of units from the contractor and be faced with members wanting to move in phases. Or you may all get your keys on the same day and be moving all together. Both ways pose their own challenges. As a community you have the opportunity to help each other through this potentially stressful time.

Before the move

● Consider which policies and agreements you want to have drafted before the community moves in and which can be left to sort out until later. These might include:

- Pets
- Common meals
- Parking
- Health and safety
- Service charge

● Consider getting all members to use the same solicitor for conveyancing. This can help to significantly reduce the work (and cost) all round.

● Think about providing each member with a welcome pack of information about your new community.

● Be prepared for delays – predicting completion dates of building projects is more an art than a science.

Planning the move

■ **Find out which members want to move on what days in an effort to reduce removal congestion.**

■ **You could consider having everyone use the same removal company – you might get a better price.**

■ **Or you could hire your own van and help each other do the move.**

■ **Think about the kids – can they help? Who is going to look after them during the move?**

■ **Think about food – plan a welcome meal for members on moving day – or get a takeaway for your exhausted**

KEY MESSAGE
All purchase and rental arrangements need to be finalised with each household before taking up their occupation

After the move

Some groups have had to move in before their Common House was finished, leading to struggles with a lack of facilities and the dangers of establishing non-sharing patterns that are hard to break later.

Snagging

After all construction projects are completed there is a 'snagging' period lasting anything up to 12 months during which the contractor is responsible for fixing any defects that come to light. This can be frustrating and distressing if you think you have just moved into your anticipated dream home.

Downsizing

It can be hard to judge how much furniture from your old house will fit when you move. Some members may feel attached to particular bits of furniture and want them to be used to furnish the Common House – which may or may not be appropriate. Having a 'Common House furnishing team' could help with decision-making and reduce any bad feeling when someone's favourite armchair is rejected.

It might be good to plan to have a 'super garage sale' a few weeks after you have all moved in to deal with all those things you never knew you had or don't know what to do with now. Some groups have a permanent swap-shop or second-hand boutique to deal with ongoing downsizing and donate anything not reused to local charity shops.

" Everything went by bike, including a dresser, chest of drawers, bookcase, dining table and chairs and two garden benches... it all feels worth it now I'm settled in to my warm eco home by the River Lune and enjoying living in the community. It was a lot more fun and less stressful than moving the traditional way! "
[Member who moved house by bike]

Build

Live

Design

Finance

Common meals

Who cooks? Who eats? Who cleans? Who pays?

Many Cohousing group members consider common meals to be the glue that holds Cohousing communities together (even if some members may only attend irregularly). A common meal may be the only time in a busy week when residents get to have real conversations with their neighbours. Common meals can make life more convenient, more economical, more practical, more interesting and more fun.

How Cohousing groups provide common meals varies widely from group to group in terms of the number of meals provided each week, the style of the meal, how the work of cooking and cleaning is organised and how the meals are paid for.

Best practice seems to be not to expect one style of food to fit all but to be flexible in how, when, where and what kind of meals are provided. It is good to discuss and plan how you want to go about providing your common meals well before you move in – and even try out some different options while you are developing your Cohousing project.

How often to eat together?

Cohousing communities generally prepare between two and five meals per week in their Common House, though this can vary from a meal every night in some groups to meals only on special occasions or on work party days in others.

Eating common meals needs to be voluntary and numbers attending will vary from meal to meal.

The meals are usually prepared by a team of two to four people for however many diners sign up for the meal in advance. In a few communities cooking is voluntary, but in most cases it is not. However, there is a good deal of variation in the way the cooking (and clean-up) responsibilities are structured. Typically, each adult ends up being involved in meal preparation and/or clean-up once every four or five weeks.

In larger groups the prospect of having to cook for forty or more people can be intimidating and can require a few more members to cope with all the tasks.

Forgebank

Advice to groups

> *Sharing is a difficult concept for many people and food can be a great 'opener' when people experience the joy of bringing and sharing a plate of food. It can be a life saver for elderly single people living alone, who miss the joy of social exchange at mealtimes, as well as providing a healthier (and cheaper) option than a takeaway meal or a ready meal for busy working families.*
>
> [Project in development]

What's your style? Cafeteria, buffet, family group, dinner party...?

Cohousers seem to prefer that a common meal feels more like eating with friends at home than eating in a school or workplace cafeteria. How this is achieved can depend on the size of the group; as a general rule, the larger the group, the greater the variety of styles of meal needed. These can include cafeteria style meals on some nights, smaller 'family style' group meals, Sunday brunches, potlucks, and pizza, curry or chippie nights. Some groups have one style of regular meal and others occasionally; others mix and match to suit.

Kids eat common meals too

Anyone who has served meals to children knows that their idea of a tasty 'balanced meal' may not be the same as an adult's. In a few of the larger communities which have a lot of children, a kid-friendly meal is sometimes or always available alongside the adult meals. It may be a completely separate meal, or a separate main dish. In most groups, children are charged a different rate. Some examples are:

- Child rate is half adult rate

- Child rate applies to children under 13

- Children under three are free

- No charge for children; parents provide a meal once a month as a 'thank you'.

KEY MESSAGE

Eating common meals needs to be voluntary and numbers attending will vary from meal to meal

Who pays?

There are many different ways that groups share the costs of common meals. Below is a list of different approaches.

- Lead cook provides and pays for the meal. No money changes hands

- A set amount is collected per person, per meal, and cooks are reimbursed up to a set budget

- Cooks set an ingredient budget for their meal. Members know the budget and menu when they sign up and pay per meal

- Cooks turn in receipts within a set limit. Total is divided between diners at that meal.

- Magic Hat – an average guide cost is set and diners pay-as-they-feel

Sorry, I can't eat that

All groups try to take into account to some degree special food needs, preferences and allergies. Almost all maintain a list of these considerations posted in the kitchen. Everyone is made aware of things like life-threatening allergies and after a while everyone remembers, without looking at the list, who can't eat dairy products or wheat and who is a vegetarian or a vegan, for example.

> *The Danes specify that to have high-functioning Cohousing, residents need to have common dinners at least twice a week in the Common House. Otherwise this thing called Cohousing is little more than a quality condominium project – it might be Cohousing-like, something inspired by Cohousing, or even something that started out as Cohousing.*
>
> [McCammant and Durrett, Creating Cohousing]

Neighbourhood Policies

Your vision in action

Whether your group is newly formed or you have been living in community for ages, at some point you will find you need a policy on this, that or the other. And let's face it, drawing up policies is not the most glamorous part of community building. But one day you may well be thankful that you took the time to think a few tricky things through.

The lengthy list of policies and agreements that some Cohousing groups have can be daunting both for a new group facing writing their own, and for a new member trying to negotiate their group's policy archive. Don't despair; there are some simple ground rules and tips you can follow. And remember, you are not the first to try and tackle writing Cohousing agreements – there are plenty of good examples around that you can borrow to get you started.

When will we need a policy on... ?

You don't need to have a full list of agreed policies at the start of your project, but there may be a few things that the initial group considers to be non-negotiable and there are obviously some things that do need to be in place from the start such as how people join, any criteria for membership, and how decisions are going to be made. There are also a few things

that are good to sort out sooner rather than later – such as having a conflict resolution process in place before you need it. Other things can be left until you can involve more members in agreeing them, and there are likely to be additional topics for which the need will only become apparent after you have moved in.

Perhaps the one important area that members will want to know about is finances. Both at the beginning, around buying or renting a property, and around paying for things like shared meals, laundry and maintenance once you move in. Most people have some understanding of the ins and outs of the property market, but many are less familiar with what a service charge might cover.

Groups differ in what they include in a service charge, but most will budget for at least the following:

- repair and maintenance of common areas;
- goods in Common House, guestrooms etc;
- water and electricity for shared facilities;
- insurance of common areas;
- gardening and landscaping work;
- group admin.

Laundry costs, guest rooms and meals are often paid for by use. Other costs can be included if it is cheaper to do it collectively.

 KEY MESSAGE
Consider instigating a 'policy lock' so that policies are not revisited until after members have moved into their Cohousing homes

What agreements do we need?

There are several issues that come up for all groups for which they need to get agreement on a policy for. Other issues will be specific to your community and its particular concerns and circumstances. You may want to be as green as possible, or address affordability, or focus on being intergenerational.

The following list may not be comprehensive, but it will give you an idea of some of the typical issues that come up that you may need agreements on:

- membership;
- decision making;
- communal meals;
- pets;
- parking;
- smoking;
- use of Common House;
- equality and diversity;
- use of guest rooms;
- conflict resolution;
- lettings policy;
- personal data;
- privacy;
- service charge.

Templates and reviews

Take your time to talk these issues through – it can be helpful to have a template that clearly shows the difference between the policy statement and the requirement for implementing it – what might be called the policy in action. This makes it easier to tweak things in the light of experience without having to revisit the headline policy. At least one group has set up a policy 'MOT' process to do this.

"To do Drawer"

In discussion about a policy it often happens that another related issue will come up. In order for this not to side-track the discussion, or for the new topic to get forgotten about, some groups note it down and put it in a virtual 'to do drawer' to be revisited at a later date.

> *Cohousing communities generally use consensus decision-making. Get training in how to do it effectively. Later, as more members join, you'll need another training to catch them up; in the interim, include some kind of internal orientation to the decision-making system as part of bringing new people on board.*
> [Tree Bresson - www.treegroup.info]

Policy Lock

One of the biggest stumbling blocks that forming groups can come across is the tendency to keep revisiting policies and agreements throughout the development stage when new members join. While this can seem very democratic and fair, it can distract from solving the number one issue that defeats groups – namely finding a site.

Some groups have instigated what they have called a policy lock – whereby once a policy has been drawn up it is agreed that it won't be revisited until after they have moved into their Cohousing homes, or even six months after they have moved in – to give time to see if it works.

This can not only free up energy for looking for a site, but can also reassure more cautious members that the group they are joining won't fundamentally change in the few years it inevitably takes to create Cohousing.

CAUTION

While policies and procedures are an essential part of any organisation, and together provide a roadmap for day-to-day operations, they are not the be all and end all of living in Cohousing. It is much easier to tie things up with rules and bureaucracy than it is to dismantle them later. Another approach some groups use is to rely on the relationships in the community and make requests of one another in the first place to see if something can be worked out before moving to "We need to get a policy about this!"

Build

Live

Finance Design

Living in Cohousing

Now the real community building work starts

Once you have recovered from moving house and got over the initial euphoria of actually having created your Cohousing bricks and mortar, there is still plenty to do. Once you have some homes, living in them – and managing and maintaining them – is probably the most important stage of all. Do this well and your group will succeed for decades to come.

There will inevitably be a communal honeymoon feel to the first months after you move in as everyone finds their feet and you try out all your new shared facilities and ideas. Running your group now carries on the good work you started in the group stage. Good organisation reduces stress, as well as wasted time, materials and money. The important thing is to avoid reinventing the wheel; there is so much collective experience out there now, which you can use and adapt, and you only need to invent if you really want to.

Managing Cohousing and all its facilities is no mean feat. You may choose to manage maintenance activities yourself with volunteers, or you may outsource this to a managing agent or partner (like a housing association). Or you could arrange for some work to be done voluntarily and pay someone to do the rest. Whatever your approach, make sure the people involved have the skills and time to do the job.

Try to remember the importance of people in all of this. Having meetings, getting agreements in place and deciding policies are essential, but these are your homes, as well as being a business. Make sure any bureaucracy you establish is there to further the aims of the group. If it doesn't, don't be afraid to throw it out.

116

Advice to groups

Sharing out the work

There is lots of work to do once you have moved in to your new community, both on setting up new communal systems and on maintaining them in the long run.

Most groups set up some sort of system of subcommittees, working groups or service teams and delegate decisions and work to them rather than trying to run everything from a Cohousing central committee. These can cover everything from finance to fun. Clear remits, budgets and delegated powers for these groups can make it easier all round and help you avoid misunderstandings and conflicts.

Car sharing

Cohousing lends itself to car sharing, either by individuals doing it informally or by the group taking a more formal approach and setting up some sort of car share scheme or car club.

In the last few years car sharing has become somewhat harder due to the rising cost and problems of accessing insurance. If you use a personal car with 'any other driver' insurance cover as a community car share/car club without telling your insurer, you run the risk of the policy being voided in the event of a significant accident.

Going down the more formal car club route has some advantages, although it may not suit small groups or work for members who need regular access to a car for work or other 'essential user' reasons.

> *We encourage members to belong to one or more sub-groups, which carry budgets, although large spends need to be ratified by the main group. In a more formal manner, we meet once a month for a 'main group meeting'.*
> [Established community]

> *It can be hard work; we are a self-managed association, so we do our own accounts. We have a laundry that we have a charge for, a service fee and other expenditures to track. We also have 14 working groups that manage and organise the site, from maintenance to fun to the nitty gritty of the business and accounts. For example, we have a garden team that maintains the external areas and a food group that organises the community meals and gets people in and cooking.*
> [Established community]

Legal matters

Cohousing communal facilities don't neatly fit into the usual boxes that authorities use. Are they some sort of impersonal premises, or are they just an extension of domestic properties? Either way you may want to take the following into account:

● **food hygiene regulations:** even if you don't need cooks to get level 1 food hygiene certificates you might want to think about basic food safety;

● **fire safety regulations:** insurers are likely to require regular checks and maintenance of fire alarms and extinguishers;

● **other Insurance requirements:** there are likely to be conditions that need to be met for building and contents insurance for communal areas;

● **landlord's responsibilities:** if you have rented properties the group will have additional legal responsibilities;

● **health and safety:** you will have a duty of care for your members safety while using your communal facilities: the easiest way to do this might be to have a H&S policy and carry out annual risk assessments;

● **Equalities Act:** if you have 25 or more members you will need to comply with the Equalities Act.

Cohousing home truths

It's not always "and they lived happy ever after in Cohousing"

Most people drawn to Cohousing are seeking a more harmonious and connected way of life than that of mainstream society. Unfortunately it can't just be wished into existence. We would not want to hide the fact that it can be hard work and sometimes the going gets tough. It can be all too easy to get carried away by the romance of it all after visiting a beautiful Cohousing project somewhere and gloss over the fact that if we want to live better lives in community we've got to do things differently and that's not always easy. Generally though things are as good as the effort you put in.

It is not easy, for example, for a group of 30+ adults to make decisions together. Meetings can be very lengthy as everyone wants their say and it can be difficult to resolve opposing views. And while there is plenty of help and advice available to help with the process of running meetings sometimes things like members' different attitudes to risk can cause real problems.

> **For the risk averse, it can be exhausting listening to a steady stream of new things to try; what's exciting for the risk tolerant is a nightmare for the risk averse. Consequently, they come to dread meetings. Going the other way, it's a drag for the risk tolerant, every time they introduce a new idea, to be offered up a steady diet of worry and caution from the risk averse – sucking the life out of the conversation. Consequently, they come to dread meetings.**
> *[communityandconsensus.blogspot.com]*

Everyone at some point has to let go of dearly held opinions for the sake of finding consensus with the group and inevitably members need to give up certain individual freedoms.

No matter how strong your group is at some point there will be conflicts between members. It might be about the management of the community, the governance of the group or anti-social behaviour from residents. Whatever its nature it's best to have a clear and transparent process in place to deal with it before the conflict occurs and discretion and sensitivity when it comes to handling it.

Advice to groups

Pioneer member syndrome

> *The trickiest part is resolving conflicts. Our conflicts policy has a starting assumption that everyone is acting out of good intentions by trying to do the best for the community. We are good people without malicious motivations and it is more likely that disagreement has arisen out of a misunderstanding, rather than deliberate wrongdoing.*
> *[Established community]*

It's almost inevitable that there will come a point when the disparity between what some members envisaged the community would be like and the reality of what it has been possible to achieve becomes clear. The pain and disappointment that this disparity can cause is likely to be felt more strongly the earlier the person joined, and perhaps most strongly by the first wave of Cohousers to move in – the 'pioneers'. There is a commonly found pattern of founders/ pioneers leaving after a couple of years – often after getting into conflict with other members and usually feeling critical of the group. It's not particularly something to worry about – it takes a certain sort of character to be a pioneer and to be able to get a venture built and up and running; it takes 'sustainers' to keep it going.
See: http://blog.utopia-britannica.org.uk/1017

Five responses to conflict

- **Ignore it** – often not a conscious choice, more a lifelong avoidance pattern.
- **Leave it** – leave the subject, leave the room, leave it to someone else, leave the group.
- **Leap in** – some people seem to thrive on conflict and may unconsciously create it.
- **Change how you feel** – conflict can be an opportunity for personal growth.
- **Use it to strengthen community** – if handled well, dealing with conflict can make a community stronger and more connected.

There are plenty of good examples for handling conflict – see the RESOURCES section of this Guide.

It might be useful to get some early practice at conflict resolution starting with a fairly minor disagreement, so that when a 'big issue' arises you already have some experience in dealing with conflict as a community.

Comings and Goings

It is a simple fact that not everyone who moves in to Cohousing stays. Why do people leave? Reasons vary, but generally it's because lives change or expectations aren't met. Some may find that the group or the location doesn't work for them the way they thought it would. Don't be too surprised when someone announces they are leaving. Dealing with turnover is part of the ongoing ebb and flow of community life.

Sustaining the community's vision

Surviving and thriving

When you've done all the hard work of developing your group, designing your scheme, getting it built, moving in, making it work, living in it... you are at some point, almost inevitably going to ask yourselves, or be asked by someone, a question to the effect of **Was it all worth it?**

What honest answer you might give will depend to a certain extent on how much the experience of community life has met your own expectations of it and partly on how realistic, robust and resilient your group vision has turned out to be in the cool reality of actually living it.

It's worth now and then doing a reality check - asking yourself as an individual, or as a group: Did we do what we said we would do? Does it still pretty much work – as a community or for you? And could it be better?

Some things in Cohousing are pretty resilient and hard to change. The architecture, for instance, is designed to foster social interaction and you might say is 'set in concrete' and it would be costly to make any major alteration to it. Legal things are pretty permanent as well: constitutions, leases, planning agreements... What can change over time by default or design is your community 'software'.

Finding a way to ensure continuity of the group's original vision and intentions is not always easy and what seems an important issue at the start of a project may change over time. Different bits of your vision will be more or less important to different members of your group. But it is likely that there will be some core statements that all of you will want to try and ensure are part of the group's lasting legacy. These may be around things such as demographic mix of membership or affordability. Some aspects of affordability

may be covered by a planning agreement with the local council if you have one and be assured 'in perpetuity'. If you want to build in some restrictions on open market sales these need to be thought through from the start and probably written in as a lease clause. But remember that housing markets change over time.

More than one intentional community has found, years down the line, that prospective members, in circumstances similar to that the next prospective members, in circumstances similar to that of the orignal founders, cannot afford to join the community at contemporary costs.

Maintaining a balanced membership may be hard. Restricting sales to particular types of people is difficult unless you have some sort of local priority staircasing built in to your advertising and letting policies or have overall age restriction on membership. It is generally true, however, that like attracts like and the sort of people who look to join you will be similar to the sort of people who are members already.

Letting out properties to others

What views might a community have on allowing households to let out their property to non-members, e.g. if there is a need to be away for a while? Communities could use such opportunities as a means to find potential future members, but they could also feel that such arrangements need careful thought and planning. Consideration could be given to the community being more centrally involved in any such lettings – such as a role in agreeing who takes up the residence – and not leaving all the matters solely to the single household by itself.

Advice to groups

> *The sense of community and connection that a group of people can cocreate is both valuable and vulnerable. It is the responsibility of each member who values the community to nourish and protect it. There may be a conflict between nourishing and protecting: nourishing can mean bringing in new fertiliser – new members with new perspectives, enthusiasms, and energy); protecting can involve not accepting risky new people. Each community must find its own balance point between risk and safety. This balance point may change over time, as the needs and strengths of the group vary.*
> [Communities Magazine #106]

Forming, storming and norming

You may come across advice on group development here and there that may be useful, but very little has been written about the group dynamics of trying to set up a new community venture.

It can be seen from experience elsewhere that some people's skills lie in being founders of new projects, while other people's skills lie in building strength into communities from what has been begun.

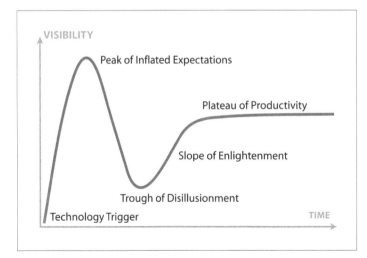

The graph above shows the pattern observed in the development of new innovations, known as the hype cycle. Originally observed in the world of hi-tech, but now being used in other areas, everyone seeing it asks: "How do you get from the peak to the plateau without going through the trough?" If you find a way do let us know!

Groups grow and change

It is OK to change your own mind. But it's a very different story when there are thirty other minds involved. To say your group will never change a decision is unrealistic. To casually reopen every decision whenever somebody thinks they've got a better idea is crazy.

It is worth developing a policy for reconsidering decisions. This might include asking members who want a decision to be reconsidered to first research the existing decision – why it was made and any background to it. It might also ask that they present new information or experiences that have arisen since the original decision was made and outline pros and cons of changing the decision – all before making a formal proposal to a meeting.

If the project has a kind of 'waiting list' of prospective members (or some form of 'associate members'), think how to include these people in particular meetings, discussions and other events

> *Those of us here, however, feel that the benefits we derive from the community outweigh the individual sacrifices. We are not all similar types of people. Some are naturally more sociable than others. Some have strongly-held, very individualistic ideas. Some love meetings, others loathe them! Some adore the chaos created by children, others find it trying. But the community way of life seems to suit us all in different ways.*
> [Established community]

Input from CLH-Accredited Advisors

CLH Facilitators and Hubs could support projects in the live stage through:

Live-in policies

Assisting with the completion of 'live-in' policies and identification of comparable policies elsewhere

Ongoing skills

Helping enable the local development of property management and maintenance skills

Participation

Participating in occasional 'community meals'

Additional facilities

Supporting with sourcing funds for additional facilities

Marmalade Lane

Support from key stakeholders

Key stakeholders (for example local government authorities; second-tier town, parish and community councils; housing associations; developers; etc.) could support projects in the LIVE stage through:

New members

Policies can be drawn up to identify new members to occupy 'affordable' units and to consider options for existing members to transfer between properties when vacancies arise.

Support for low income rental households

Supporting applications from Cohousers for housing benefit, where the Cohousing rental costs and service charges are within local housing allowance rates.

Calculation of service charges

Housing associations or local authorities may help with the presentation of management and maintenance costs within the Cohousing service charge rates.

New Ground

Threshold Centre, Dorset

Design

Basic principles of Cohousing site designs and layouts

Build

Live

Design

Finance

Design requirements by project stages

Group tasks	Design requirements
Agreeing a project's vision	Agreeing the key focus of the project: • Multi-generational or senior households • New-build or retrofit • Desired eco-standards

Site tasks	Design requirements
Assessing sites: initial design concept(s)	• Site assessments and feasibility considerations • Indicative ideas of site layout according to points of access

Plan tasks	Design requirements
Final design: placement of facilities	• Completion of all dwelling designs • Completion of Common House designs and other facilities • Agreement of design for landscaping and open spaces

Build tasks	Design requirements
Construction: internal and external quality control	• Oversight by project designer of construction quality • Choice of landscape materials

Live tasks	Design Requirements
Occupation: first use of domestic and communal spaces	Assessment of design performance in 'snagging' period

Sources of Information and Advice

Books which include information on Cohousing design

- **Cohousing** *K McCamant and C Durrett* 1994, 2011 ISBN 0898155398 (core background material on central concepts and examples)

- **Creating Cohousing** *K McCamant and C Durrett* 2011 ISBN 9780865716728

- **Thinking About Cohousing** *Martin Field* Diggers and Dreamers Publications 2004 ISBN 0951494570

- **Designing the Cohousing Common House** *G Kim* 2006 www.schemataworkshop.com (design details on Common House locations and contents)

- **We are in Charge** *M Brenton* 1998 Policy Press, ISBN 9781861341334

- **The Cohousing Approach to Lifetime Neighbourhoods** *M Brenton* 2008, Housing Learning and Improvement network, Factsheet 29 www.housingcare.org/downloads/kbase/3140.pdf

- **Senior Cohousing** *M Brenton* 2013 Joseph Rowntree Trust ISBN 9781859359266

- **The Senior Cohousing Handbook** *Charles Durrett* New Society Publications 2009 ISBN 0865716110

- **Cohousing in Britain – a Diggers & Dreamers Review** 2011 ISBN 9780954575731 (the first phase of Cohousing implementations in the UK, and chapter on eco-design)

- **Low Impact Living** *P Chatterton* 2014 ISBN 9781933128139 (focused description of LILAC eco-project)

- **Creating Community-Led and Self-Build Homes** *Martin Field* 2020 ISBN 9781447344391 (chapter on design challenges to 'Cohousing neighbourhoods')

- **Community Enhanced Design – Cohousing and other high-functioning neighbourhoods** *Charles Durrett* 2022 ISBN 9781119897705 (www.cohousingco.com)

- **Grounded patterns: creating a socio-spatial language for residents' participation in cohousing landscapes** *Aimee Louise Felstead and Kevin Thwaites* 2021 (Proceedings of XXVIII International Seminar on Urban Form, Glasgow)

Websites which cover design for Cohousing

- UK Cohousing Network www.cohousing.org.uk

- New Ground www.owch.org.uk/resources

- US Cohousing www.cohousing.org

- German approaches to 'CoHousing' and other collaborative housing projects www.cohousing-inclusive.net/the-book

- Housing our Ageing Population Panel for Innovation (HAPPI) – www.housinglin.org.uk/Topics/browse/Design-building/Neighbourhoods/ (information on and examples of Lifetime Neighbourhoods and 'Senior' projects across Europe)

Core principles

Does Cohousing need a special design?

Cohousing projects have a core intention to promote a balance between personal privacy and a common, shared identity within a deliberately crafted neighbourhood environment.

The key principles of their designs are focused upon:

- The physical form layout of neighbourhoods make deliberate use of architectural and design features that can maximise opportunities for social contact and strengthen local connections within the neighbourhood.

- Self-contained accommodation is supplemented by significant common facilities and spaces, of which a 'Common House' is a crucial setting for shared activities.

- Each neighbourhood is of a scale that will underpin sustainable relationships across the neighbourhood: between 20 and 50 adults is seen as an optimum scale (plus children, if the project is family-based).

Cohousing-style development is well-suited to a low-rise but high-density provision, both in new-build settings and in rehabilitated buildings, as its intentions are for residents to build relationships from the myriad ways they could come into daily contact with each other.

The design of a Common House as a key site for communal activities should include sufficient space for all residents of the neighbourhood to be able to meet together. Its location in the neighbourhood should be at the heart of where residents will naturally move around.

> " The centrality to Cohousing neighbourhoods of their Common House is fundamental in maximising opportunities to become more familiar with neighbours and fellow members and will be at the core of the community's identity... The Common House and other common facilities are the heart of a Cohousing community "
> [McCamant and Durrett, 2011]

The movement of traffic in or through the neighbourhood areas should be minimised, making maximum use of car-free and pedestrianised environments (another benefit of this could be reduced expenditure on the costs of roads and hard surfaces).mln larger sites that could accommodate more dwellings than the optimum size noted above, opportunities will arise to create more than one Cohousing project, each with its own separate common facilities. (Examples from Scandinavian urban areas show clusters of Cohousing units within wider residential developments. Lancaster Cohousing is in the process of supporting new Senior Cohousing provision by the side of the previously developed Forgebank Cohousing scheme.)

The typical facilities that Cohousing communities create within Common Houses and other communal spaces include:

- kitchen and dining facilities

- sitting rooms or spaces for relaxation

- laundry facilities

- guest rooms

- workshops or office spaces

- meeting rooms

- play spaces

- equipment stores

Distinctive comparison

This grid compares Cohousing design with contemporary mainstream neighbourhood design

Cohousing	Mainstream
The architecture of the neighbourhood is intended to maximise opportunities for intentional and incidental social contact, to bring neighbours into visual and verbal contact with each other.	The focus is upon maximising household privacy above other contacts. Consideration could be given to incorporating a remote view or surveillance of public or semi-public areas.
The size of a community is crucial – large enough for people to be absent without it being problematic, but small enough for people to be able to establish proper relationships with their neighbours (i.e. under 50 adults per scheme).	There is little appreciation of how the size or scale of the built development will impact on future relationships between a neighbourhood's residents. Policies to increase site densities do not stimulate a sensitive understanding of the impact on local identity.
The design and location of a Common House/building is considered fundamental for creating community identity. It should invite people into it as they pass on their way to and from home and be large enough for all residents to meet together at one time.	Common or shared facilities are not usually planned for local relationships, but for wider impersonal areas. Communal facilities are not seen as valuable in assisting the development of local relationships.
Neighbourhoods use garden and green spaces as external and leisure spaces to encourage residents to mix. Vehicle use is kept to an edge of the overall site.	There is a predominance of car use with vehicle access to all individual properties. Significant amounts of land are devoted to public roads and hard-standing surfaces.
Internal spaces where people spend a significant amount of time (like kitchen areas) are positioned deliberately to promote visual connections with communal spaces and activities outside.	Prevalent UK housing designs accentuate the privacy of internal uses away from contact with neighbours.
Any private garden areas are on a modest scale, since importance is given to providing substantial other communal green space(s).	Designs usually focus on private entertainment with some public open space. There is little consideration of 'communal' spaces dedicated to a set of local households.
Parking areas and play facilities are placed close to where other daily activities take place, to increase community contact between all members.	Parking and play facilities are located where it is hoped they will not intrude into others' relaxation. Facilities can be very one-dimensional and focused by age group.

Build

Live

Design

Finance

Site types, orientation and access

How to make your site work for Cohousing

Use the point of access into the Cohousing site to start opportunities for social contacts between residents.

The main access into sites (such as indicative square or rectangular sites) will channel access to other common spaces and private dwellings in the areas beyond.

See examples of access into indicative sites in 'Basic Principles of Cohousing Design' – the complementary PowerPoint/PDF presentation prepared for this Guide (please note the text in the diagrams below is fully visible within the presentation).

Basic principles of Cohousing design

Can be downloaded from:

www.communityledhomes.org.uk/resources

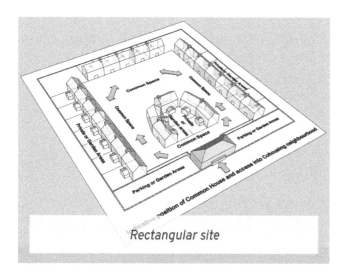

Rectangular site

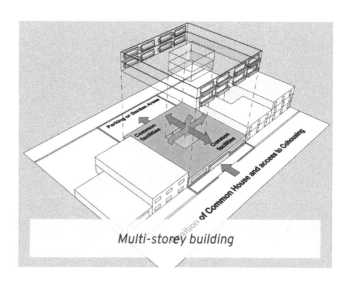

Multi-storey building

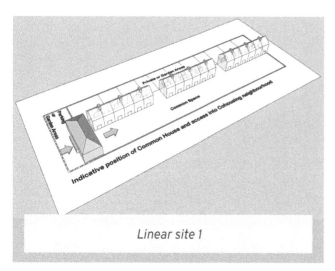

Linear site 1

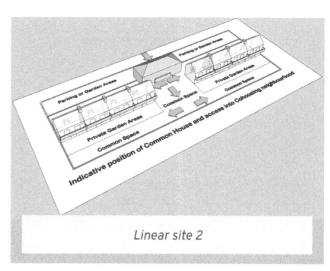

Linear site 2

Space Requirement

The use of space in Cohousing projects underpins the attraction that many find in their communities. Using space wisely needs a clear understanding of what to do in practice.

On a new site, the optimum number of adults noted above, translated into a number of new-build properties, is likely to require a site of between one and two acres, depending on the final number of households. Yet sites have rarely become available to suit a prescribed number – it is more usual that groups must respond to what could be available and then see how to craft a suitable Cohousing design out of potentially unpromising beginnings.

Example: Forgebank, Lancashire

Description

A long linear site, straddling the river edge

Comment

Accessed from one end of the site; minimal parking provision; pedestrian walkways through the site

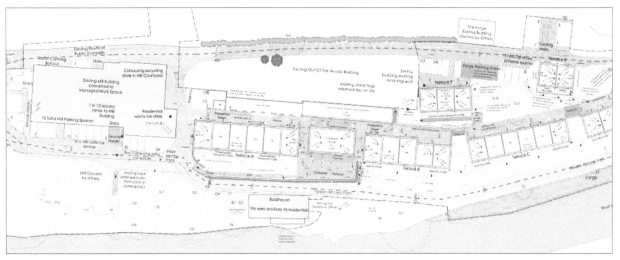

Placement of the Common House and the dwellings

Position the Common House closest to the main point of entering in order for this to be integral to residents' daily activities and encourage contact with each other. The extent and range of facilities located in or around the Common House will depend on the choices of each community, but could include:

- internal and external seating areas;

- kitchen space and dining areas;

- laundry facilities;

- guest rooms;

- space to collect mail/deliveries;

- children's play space;

- workshop/equipment stores;

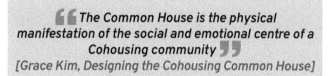
The Common House is the physical manifestation of the social and emotional centre of a Cohousing community
[Grace Kim, Designing the Cohousing Common House]

Locate the private residences so that they are oriented towards each other within the site and accessed from inside the site, rather than from peripheral roads. Properties could be low-rise dwellings, or maisonettes or apartments, including above the Common House. Consider the possibility of internal semi-public areas like wide glazed corridors as a congenial means of entry into the private units.

Utilise designs that could permit private expansion of internal space, where feasible.

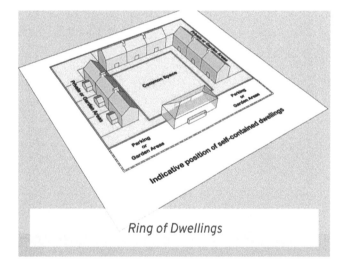
Ring of Dwellings

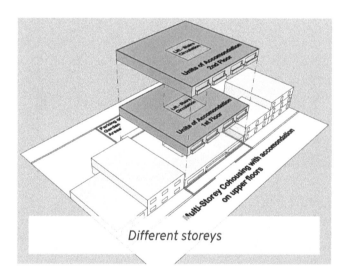
Different storeys

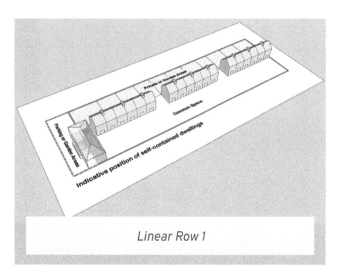
Linear Row 1

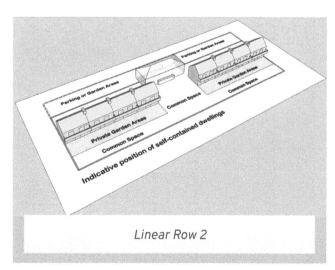
Linear Row 2

Prime point of access

The central location of the Common House, and its orientation as the prime point of site access and conviviality, is a long-established feature of Cohousing practice.

> **" The prominently located Common House is the community's central meeting place, where children and adults get together. This is clearly the neighbourhood's backbone as informal talks and meetings take place here... [plus] a kitchen equipped for cooking for the whole community, and a large activities room "**
> [Trudeslund, Denmark]

Examples of the location of Common Houses on Cohousing sites

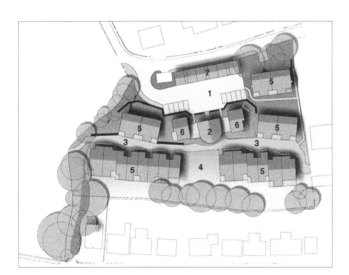

Springhill, Gloucestershire

Description
Steep sloping rectangular site, close to the town centre

Comment
Parking at the top of the site; buildings radiate around the Common House and down the slope

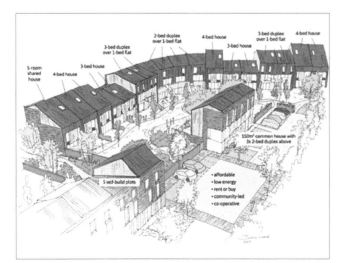

Chapeltown (ChaCo), Yorkshire

Description
Triangular inner-city site, orienting households away from traffic and external environments

Comment
A mix of property types and positions, with Common House adjacent to parking areas

Common House interiors and shared facilities

- Common Houses can be built from new, or reconditioned from existing properties

- Should be designed to be the core point of community contact and interactions

- Should be large enough for all members to congregate and socialise together

- Should include communal kitchens and dining areas and other cosy places in which to relax

- Will be a key place to provide mailboxes, laundry facilities and other work and play spaces

- Could also be the place to site any guest room(s)

In a 2022 presentation to UKCN Grace Kim listed common pitfalls to avoid when designing a common house:

- Poor attention to acoustics and surfaces in dining areas

- Insufficient storage of dining tables and chairs

- Glare of lighting in dining areas

- Dining areas being too small

- Kitchen areas not able to provide for community meals

- Insufficient storage for personal and community needs

Here is an indicative plan for a modest common house of about 130 square metres which will seat 30 to 40 people at meals.

- The kitchen window is aligned with the walkway outside to maximise sight-lines inside and out

- Patio doors at the far end to wider outdoor spaces

- Other facilities, floors or elements can be added or considered, as desired

Springhill Common House

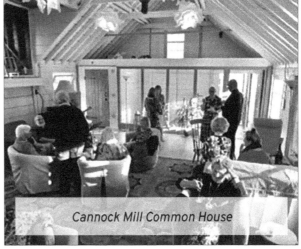

Cannock Mill Common House

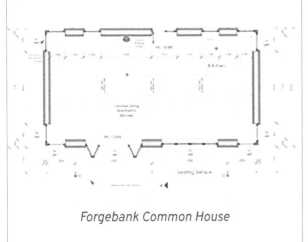

Forgebank Common House

Forgebank Common House

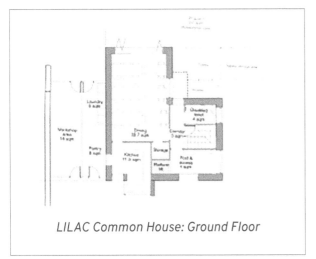

LILAC Common House: Ground Floor

LILAC Common House: First Floor

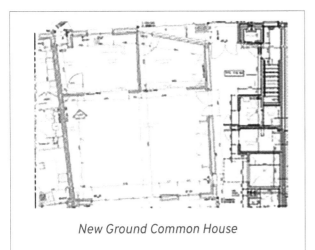

New Ground Common House

New Ground Common House

Garden areas and parking provision

Outdoor space in a Cohousing community

What gardens can we have?

Cohousing design recognises that households would like some private external space for their own leisure use but acknowledges that this need not be extensive. Wider opportunities for substantial communal uses of open spaces and green areas across the site will compensate for these smaller private areas.

Different communities want, or have acquired, space for allotments, food cultivation and other ecological uses, alongside the usual space for dwellings. Consideration will need to be given to the management of non-residential areas and other open land, and how this connects with other aspects of the Cohousing community's life.

Vehicle-free environments and parking provision

Cohousing neighbourhoods use their site's space most creatively if vehicle use can be acutely minimised within the site. Restricting cars from entering into a site, and to parking at or along its edges, will save land from needing to be unnecessarily given up to traffic and allow more green space and opportunities for private and communal leisure activities.

Ideal places to park vehicles will be just inside a site's main entrance, not driving into a site to stand by individual properties. (Cannock Mill has some spaces by properties and some by the Common House due to its steep site.)

Parking provision in a dedicated place can also promote incidental social interaction in walking between homes and vehicles, especially if the parking is close to the Common House. The parking area can also be a site for charging points if electric vehicles are being favoured.

Access into a site for emergency purposes does not require emergency vehicles to park immediately by each building, only that crews and emergency personnel can access all parts of the site with their equipment.

Forgebank

Advice to groups

Car ownership

As people live in Cohousing, they tend to find they need fewer cars than they first expected – more car sharing takes place and parking needs are reduced.

Senior Cohousing projects could have less car ownership than family-based Cohousing projects and accordingly plan for reduced parking provision.

Example: New Ground

Description
A rectangular urban site with street-fronted entrance by the Common House and apartments on three floors

Comment
Communal garden areas; flower beds to ground floor units and balconies upstairs; ten on-site parking spaces, requiring payment from residents

Sustainable design considerations

Inclusivity and flexibility

- Cohousing sites, spaces and dwellings need to be accessible for all mobility needs – including fitting lifts in multi-storey buildings.

- Dwellings must be adaptable and flexible to meet changes in personal circumstances – utilising the key principles of 'lifetime homes' (**www.lifetimehomes.org.uk**) to create properties usable to residents at all stages in their lives and health.

- Ensure dwellings can be accessed and visited by all residents to remove impediments to natural friendships and reciprocal visits.

- Use colours/contrasts/choice of materials, surfaces and furniture to assist personal navigations around the site and within its properties – especially within the Common House and other communal facilities.

- Incorporate electronic/web-based connections across the site, and especially within the common facilities, that can assist audibility at community events, meal-times, etc.

Give attention early

Attention given to inclusive design at the planning stage can focus on ensuring that flexibility has been incorporated into the facilities on-site.

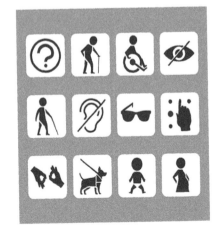

Eco issues

Even the most urban site can combine eco-design principles and sustainability concepts to maximise a beneficial impact on the natural environment, such as:

- sustainable construction techniques – use of low-emission and zero-carbon materials, combined with suitable construction methods;

- PassivHaus design – the orientation of buildings to balance passive solar gains with maximising daylight in rooms, use of photovoltaics and other measures;

- site ecology – enhancing local bio-diversity with 'green roofs', rainwater harvesting and water recycling, which can be part of the site's sustainable drainage system (SuDS) strategy and reduce water consumption;

- localised district heating networks – generating heat centrally and distributing it through insulated pipes to individual premises (also known as heat networks or teleheating); the system can reduce operating bills and lower carbon/waste emissions;

- community gardens – rainwater harvesting as a simple way to water site gardens and allotments;

Designing to meet low-energy demands can take a 'building fabric' first approach, using low or zero carbon technologies on site to achieve reduced demand for space heating while still delivering thermally comfortable and efficient properties

The Forgebank and Cannock Mill projects have both achieved building standards to 'PassivHaus' accreditations.

Advice to groups

Welsh Assembly Initiative

The Welsh government adopted its One Wales: One Planet policy in 2011:
wales.gov.uk/docs/desh/publications/
090521susdev1wales1planeten.pdf
to support new ideas for people to live and work on their own land. See also the One Planet Council
www.oneplanetcouncil.org.uk
that has been established to support applicants of such schemes.

Example: LILAC, Yorkshire

Description

A confined inner-city, ex-school site

Comment

Straw-bale construction; SuDS; small allotments

The One Planet Living framework

At the core of the framework are ten simple principles that cover all aspects of social, environmental and economic sustainability, ranging from 'health and happiness' to 'zero carbon energy'.

The ten One Planet Living principles:

 Health and happiness

 Equity and local economy

 Culture and community

 Land and nature

 Sustainable water

 Local and sustainable food

 Travel and transport

 Materials and products

 Zero waste

Zero carbon energy

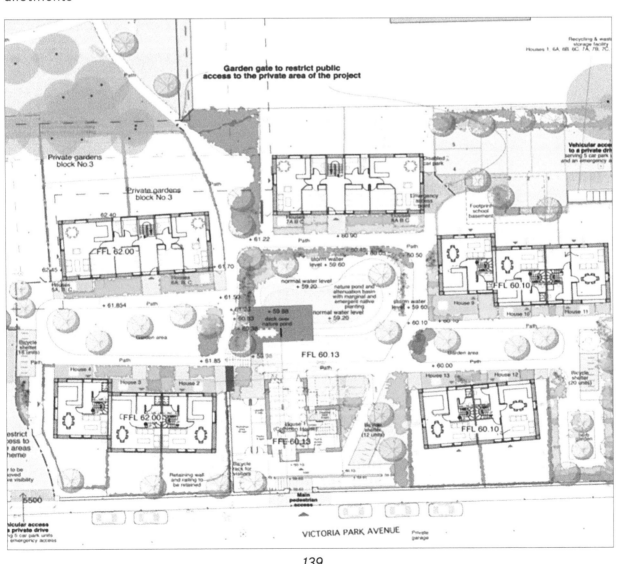

Input from CLH-Accredited Advisors

CLH Facilitators and Hubs could support projects through:

Professional appointments

Assisting with identifying suitable designers familiar with Cohousing principles and projects

Project management

Commissioning a project manager to help the project through all design-related tasks and appraisals

Links between projects

Helping groups communicate with other Cohousing groups and projects undertaking similar design considerations

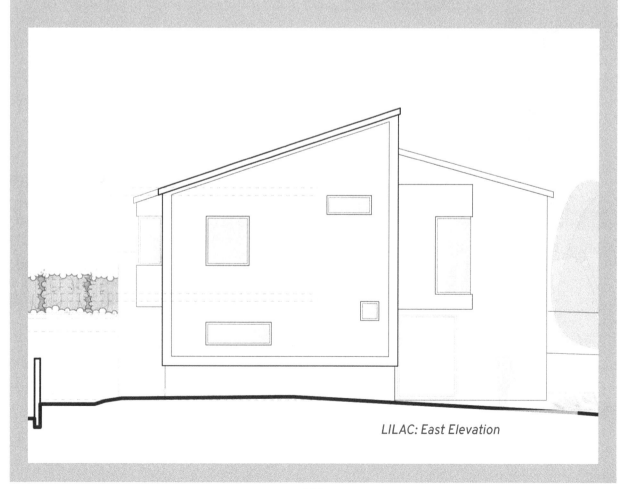

LILAC: East Elevation

Support from key stakeholders

Key stakeholders (for example local authorities, parish councils, housing associations developers etc) could support projects through:

Local design policies

Local planning authorities could include a clear identification of Cohousing principles in their codes and standards for built and landscaped architecture, including policies for:

- layouts of sites;

- vehicle-free environments;

- Common House(s) and shared facilities;

- access to private dwellings from inside the neighbourhood (i.e. not street-fronting);

- on-site facilities (energy, allotments, etc...)

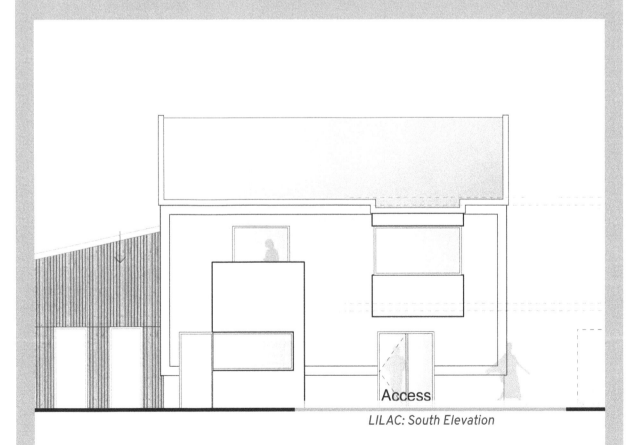

Access

LILAC: South Elevation

Marmalade Lane Cohousing, Cambridgeshire

Finance

A summary of the funding required at each stage of Cohousing project development

Build

Live

Finance Design

Key project pipeline tasks

A summary of the finances required at different stages of a Cohousing project's development

Group tasks	Financial requirements
Initial meeting(s) between core initiators	Any small sums to cover expenses for initial meetings – room hire, publicity, printing
Fee proposal(s) agreed with Hubs/Facilitators	Funds to cover agreed CLH support services (e.g. from 'CLH start-up' grants, if available)
Legal incorporation	1. Legal fees 2. Registration fees

Site tasks	Financial requirements
Initial concept(s) – technical and social	1. Potential fees for indicative designs or ideas 2. Project manager fees (if the group makes early appointment)
Feasibility studies and financial modelling	External fees for any rudimentary works or services
Land identified or acquired	Potential deposit to secure development opportunity
Site acquisitions	Terms of purchase/lease of identified site or other property

Plan tasks	Financial requirements
Detailed design – technical, social and common facilities	1. Design and professional fees 2. Project Manager fees (if appointed)
Planning permissions and agreements	1. Planning and Building Regs fees payable to local authority 2. Funds required at stages set by formal legal agreements
Build costs finalised	Other professional fees

Build tasks	Financial requirements
Development finance secured	Capital finance to cover all phases of construction works
Homes under construction/ property renovated	Payment of construction works at agreed times according to contract

Live tasks	Financial requirements
Sales, rents and service charges	1. Members purchase property/equity to redeem building loan 2. Partners pay required costs for rental units and agree rent levels 3. Rates of rent and service charges set to meet management and maintenance costs
Neighbourhood policies – meals; laundry, etc	Funds from households to meet individual use of facilities

New Ground

Potential sources of finance

Public sector funds

Capital funds might be obtainable through a project's support from, or partnership with, local authorities or local housing associations but this should not be expected simply because a Cohousing scheme has a 'community-led' label. As noted below, public grant to help meet capital construction costs is likely to be tied to the scheme providing units of 'affordable housing' over and above the levels demanded by local planning policy. (There may be a calculation that scheme costs attributable to 'affordable' units could be met by a household's welfare benefits payments in the future, which ultimately come via the public sector; this will require careful consideration within any business plan assumptions to avoid the project being assessed as over-reliant on the public purse.)

Private sector funds

It is possible that core finance for a Cohousing project could be the single key benefit that a project's external partner brings to the scheme – for example, funds that could be secured by a local housing association or an established property developer/housebuilder. It is more likely, however, that the project will need to obtain finance directly from lenders in the finance and banking sector, who can be persuaded to issue loan finance that will need to be repaid at the end of construction, either by finding alternative loans or by sums of finance that will ultimately come from member-households via lump-sum payments, mortgage finance or something similar.

Funds from Cohousing households

Projects based on a funding model with high levels of household ownership on scheme completion may have already started a 'membership investment' arrangement, whereby pre-determined amounts of finance are supplied by members at pre-set periods.

At times, some member-households with significant levels of personal assets could be ready to offer this to the project and be repaid at a later date. This can be invaluable in providing a positive cash-flow to meet expenses as they are incurred, but it is not advisable to rely on just a few members to bankroll a much larger sum than they may be obliged to pay as an individual member.

> **There is a perception that Cohousing does not need public support because it has its own capital**
> [Section 106 expert]

Some Mutual Home Ownership schemes can require households to purchase a basic amount of equity from the MHO organisation and could include a percentage of the agreed equity as an early or 'up-front' payment.

> **The Mutual Home Ownership model was a crucial component, as vital as the scale and size of the development in supporting a sustainable community**
> [Group in development]

Funds from the Social Investment sector

Social investment sector lenders are increasingly interested in supporting suitable collaborative housing and Cohousing schemes (see Details of potential lenders later in this FINANCE section) This is most likely to be in the form of short-term loans for construction purposes, and repayable on the finish of those works. Some longer term loans might be obtained that would be gradually repaid from the community's future income, such as from rental receipts.

Is 'sweat equity' possible in Cohousing schemes?

'Sweat equity' is the term commonly given to the time and effort that a project's members put into a project to assist its development. It is not equivalent to cash but it might be a component in calculating the sum that individual households will pay for a Cohousing dwelling. The time and effort put into a scheme by members could be the basis for a discount of the final costs to be met by the incoming household although some caution will be required in calculating any final discounts on prices from just undertaking basic administrative jobs.

In some Cohousing projects, there could be a deliberate use of 'self-built' construction work being undertaken by the members. This could be translated into a notional 'equity' that is used in determining the price placed on a Cohousing unit. The value of such 'sweated' contributions in reducing construction costs of the Common House will be realised in lower project costs as a whole, rather than in lower costs for any single household.

A project's overall final expenses are likely to be the determining factor for how much (if any) 'sweat equity' can be allocated to member households.

Income from service charges

This will not be available to cover any of the basic construction costs. Service charges are what will apply after occupation to meet ongoing maintenance and repair costs.

Are funds from community shares a viable option?

Proposals for raising funds through 'community shares' are increasingly being considered by community-led housing schemes. A good source of information can be found at: http://communityshares.org.uk/resources/ handbook

A key objective of some of these funds is to assist projects that are established for wider social benefit, not only projects that are established just for their own members. Some community share schemes will require voting rights to be given to investors. **Be cautious, therefore**, with hopes that crowd-sourced or community share finance might provide funds to cover the long-term costs of Cohousing projects, if the requirement to give external investors ongoing voter rights means a lack of autonomy and control by the actual Cohousing group.

Radical Routes (a network of housing and worker co-ops and social centres working for social change in the UK) has devised a 'loan stock' system for mutual co-ops and other similar organisations to attract investment without extending voting rights to the investors. In a 'mixed-tenure' project, the use of such funds could require them to be focused just on affordable housing units, as this is the element of the project that could be seen to be of benefit to the wider community, and not just to single members. It might be feasible to set up a scheme to secure short-term funds to meet immediate construction expenses, provided it is to be repaid on completion of the build works. It is also possible that share-based income could be sourced by another body that is committed to helping a Cohousing project, such as the Cohousing/co-op project at Lowfield Green being supported by finance from YorSpace, some of which has been crowdsourced to assist its wider support for the CLH sector.

For further information on Mutual Home Ownership Society (MHOS) finances, see: https://ukmhos.weebly.com

Build

Live

Design

Finance

Just getting started costs something

First meeting(s) between core initiators

These could involve some general and minor meeting expenses. Some small grants might be available from the local authority to help new projects in the first 'start-up' phase.

Fee proposal(s) agreed with Hubs/ Facilitators

Groups could discuss with CLH-Hubs the opportunity for the Hubs to help them submit more extensive 'start up' grant applications that could then be used to engage the Hubs to provide more substantial support.

Legal incorporation

There will be some level of registration fee involved in a Cohousing project registering a new identity, and a small level of annual fee for certain forms of incorporation – such as the fees required by Companies House.

Legal fees a group could pay to its legal advisor are likely to be more substantial, but these could be reduced if projects make use of the work and information available within the CLH sector and the CLH-Hubs to minimise unnecessary expense of local advisors feeling they must be paid to reinvent a perfectly serviceable wheel.

Cannock Mill

Advice to groups

Funding pre-development

Some schemes set their members an internal membership fee as a way of building up a small fund to cover initial incidental expenses – room hire/leaflets/website etc.

For more substantial pre-development costs – including the fees for some first professional advice – projects could use private loans from members that are then accepted as deposits on Cohousing dwellings at a later date.

Access to funds to help a project through the formative and pre-development stages, working up its scheme into a credible property development proposal, might be a key reason a group seeks an external partner like a housing association or property developer.

Before entering into such a partnership, it is important to make sure that the group members and external partner are clear about the details of the partnership arrangement, specifically in relation to the amount of risk each party takes on and how the scheme will be apportioned. It is common for a partner that takes on a greater risk to be rewarded with a larger share of the scheme ownership or the economic outcomes (the profit!). Details such as these need to be made clear in any such partnership agreement.

A Cohousing project should not envisage being able to secure much financial support from the public sector (including any of the national bodies providing housing development grants) if it is not committed to providing some affordable dwellings within its final outputs.

Threshold Centre

Build

Live

Design

Finance

Site: Cost considerations for site acquisition

Feasibility studies and financial modelling

The size of most Cohousing projects will inevitably trigger the need for their planning applications to meet local policy requirements for the delivery of a mix of tenures. Anyone carrying out financial modelling of the feasibility of such schemes on identified sites (with likely identified prices) needs to properly understand the implications of what a scheme will be expected to provide and fund from its own resources.

National planning requirements of new residential development are contained in formal regulations such as the National Planning Policy Framework (NPPF) in England and Wales and the National Planning framework in Scotland. These set out how residential developments can be obliged to provide a certain percentage of the final dwellings as 'affordable units'. With the NPPF, this has usually been for schemes of ten or more units, but local policies can vary, and the demands applied to different kinds of sites – such as some 'brownfield' sites, or sites to be developed under 'permitted development' regulations – can vary at times.

Planning frameworks in England, Scotland and Wales are continually being 'reformed' and all groups should bring themselves up-to-date with the outcomes that local and national policies desire from new residential development.

Local planning policies may set additional descriptions of what 'affordable' might mean in a specific locality, in terms of 'affordable' or 'social' rented units or low-cost home ownership tenures.

The position on whether or not public grant could help meet costs of new development (like the grants sought by housing associations and registered providers) is that this will only be supported for the percentage of proposed 'affordable' units above the local planning authority's policy minimum (e.g. if the local policy is that at least 30% of all final units must be 'affordable' ones, public grant would only be available towards units additional to the 30%).

The basic expectation is that all the project's costs will need to be met by receipts and income that the total development will secure. This will include receipts from the sale of properties to households or the purchase of units by a housing association, or other capitalised receipts based on agreed calculations of future rental income streams. This is a common element of the risks that property developers assess in new schemes.

Paying the 'policy' price

Some Cohousing projects might wish to consider obtaining an exemption from the full demands of local planning policies by claiming that there are all-round financial constraints on their project that may prevent it being fully policy-compliant – akin to the way that other private sector housebuilders have sought exemptions.

A main guide here is that government has clearly stated that payment of an unrealistically high price for a site should not, in itself, be an acceptable excuse for a proposed development not meeting the local planning authority's policies in full.

Notwithstanding that possible stance, it will be a persuasive position for Cohousing projects to have when courting external support if they can state a clear intent to provide for households with a range of incomes and to provide units that will meet local planning and housing policies in full.

Site acquisitions

The basic level of funds needed to purchase land or buildings for any residential development project can be calculated by:

- working backwards from the scheme's potential outcomes and anticipated value;

- deducting the anticipated costs (including an element of profit);

- concluding what price could be paid for the site or property from the funds that remain.

In other words, the purchase price of land or property should be considered in the light of all the other costs the scheme might incur as it totals up all the elements required to meet the group's objectives and comply with local planning requirements. Sometimes this exercise is termed 'residual land valuation'.

This approach is not always taken when sites are valued and there are clear instances where the 'hope-value' that a land or property owner has for a site or existing building (at times quite obstinately) becomes an obstacle to achieving the economic returns needed to meet local policy objectives for dwellings and tenures. Groups should be prepared in their negotiations with land or property owners to explain in detail how they arrived at their estimation of likely property costs and receipts, in order to justify the rationale of their offer for the land or property under consideration.

> **❝We had to do a bit of juggling with selling properties to raise the money to purchase. There was some lending from within the group while waiting for properties to sell.❞**
> *[Group in development]*

Comparison of budget sums

Groups could consider different levels of budgets for their chosen route to acquire a site or property:

- **funds to purchase land or property outright, at an early stage of a project;**
- **funds to cover the costs of preparing an 'options' agreement to frame the completion of a future site or property purchase, subject to the precise terms of future planning approvals;**
- **funds to meet the terms of a deferred purchase agreement (e.g. to finalise the site or property purchase on completion of the finished dwellings).**

Forgebank

Build

Live

Design

Finance

Finalisation of all design and build costs

Once a suitable site has been identified, or some existing property found to renovate or remodel, the project's business plan becomes crucial as it should provide a clear summary of the funds that will be required to undertake the design and build works envisaged.

Funds will be needed to cover:

- fees to complete all necessary designs and plans;

- fees for other professional agents such as legal advisors, architectural services, financial advisors and surveyors;

- the costs of any further feasibility studies or assessments (such as ground conditions or environment considerations) required to explore the desired site or property and contribute to the final planning application(s);

- regulatory fees payable to the local authority for submitting the planning and building regulation applications (this will depend in part on the size of the Cohousing scheme and its number of dwellings);

- ongoing fees payable to the project manager if one is already engaged by the group.

Having funds to meet these expenses (even if they are being met by an external partner and will be added to the project's bill on scheme completion!) is a core demand at this stage of the project.

Estimation of capital funds

The final and crucial element of work at this stage is to confirm what funds will be required for the construction works – the 'capital' funding required to pay for the build programme.

The work of the project's quantity surveyor here is of paramount importance in finalising a proposed budget for undertaking all construction works, including notions of how the properties will be valued on completion – always a matter of importance to funders!

That indicative budget can be subject to further change in line with quotes received from potential contractors within the project's tendering and appointment process.

The phrase 'value engineering' is a term used here to denote any required modifications to the proposed budget ("the substitution of materials and methods with less expensive alternatives, without sacrificing functionality") to alter or amend items within the construction works in order to leave the final works budget and costs within the level of funds that the Cohousing group can secure to pay for those works.

> **The main hurdle is obtaining funding especially for the initial phases of feasibility and planning**
> [CLH-Hub]

Grants and loans

In the main, public grant funds will only be available to assist a housing project if its 'affordable' outcomes will be greater than the local planning policy requires.

Cohousing projects that propose a mix of tenures in compliance with local planning policies and in which the proposed 'affordable housing' units will only meet the minimum requirements of local planning policy may not be able to secure any public grant contribution.

Projects focused on 'Mutual Home Ownership' arrangements may be able to secure public grant funds towards some costs, by virtue of the way their shared equity arrangements could meet local definitions of an affordable tenure. The likelihood of grant support will, however, still reflect whether or not the scheme will provide more affordable units than the local authority's minimum policy requirement.

There are some minor caveats to this – a public sector body could access funds to help meet unusual expenses (such as out-of-the-ordinary costs for site works) but not for core building expenses. Some authorities might contribute finances by virtue of wider policies to support community-led initiatives; the Senior Cohousing project in Lancaster is being supported in this way.

All groups should nevertheless recognise that even if public grant funds can be obtained by their scheme, there will still be a need to obtain other capital funds to meet at least 50% of the project and construction costs.

Loan finance then becomes a key consideration

- Is it to be a short-term loan (for example to provide cash to meet payments to an on-site contractor) likely to be redeemed by payments from Cohousing occupants when the construction is completed?

- Is it a long-term loan (to provide funds for rental units) which will be redeemed over the following years through rental income from the occupied dwellings?

Details of potential lenders lenders from the 'social finance' sector

The bodies noted below all provide forms of loans for CLH proposals (some also small grants). All are regulated by the Financial Conduct Authority.

Not all lenders lend funds on the same terms – groups will need to consider what could be most suitable for their own project

www.cafonline.org/charities/ borrowing/social-investment/ community-led-housing

www.charitybank.org

www.triodos.co.uk

www.ecology.co.uk

www.unity.co.uk

Build

Live

Design

Finance

Build: Capital construction costs

Acquiring the development finance

The funds that groups will need for the construction stage of their projects will be similar across the different kinds of Cohousing schemes.

The main source of capital finance could be any combination of:

- loan finance from private banks or social investment lenders;

- possible public finance (e.g. from the local authority or from the relevant national body providing housing development grants or loans);

- private funds (including household mortgages) supplied at specified times and amounts by individual members;

- loan finance from private banks or social investment lenders.

All the funds necessary to complete the construction works should be firmly secured before commitment is given to start the construction contracts on-site. This may mean having additional arrangements in place for an appropriate level of liquidity (cash!) to be on hand to meet the contractual payments due for each phase of the building activities. This could be a 'bridging loan' designed for this purpose.

With judicious financial management, it is not impossible that there could be a surplus of receipts and other income over costs and expenditure – especially if construction costs have been kept within budget and the final valuations of completed units turn out to be buoyant. Groups would do well, however, not to rely on any anticipated excess profit from their scheme – it will be achievement enough if its anticipated resources can cover all the incurred expenses!

Homes under construction or property under renovation

The project's procedures for paying contractors will need to be agreed by all parties. It is usual for construction contractors to require payment at various points in the construction work. The amount charged should be proportional to the amount of work that has been completed to an acceptable standard. The Cohousing group will need to assign someone to assess the value of the works completed at each point in order to determine whether the payments requested by the contractors are appropriate. It is common for the amount to be negotiated at each stage as the contractor's opinion of 'completed to an acceptable standard' may not match the customer's. A suitable person for this task could be the group's project manager, a clerk of works or a quality surveyor.

Once all the building works are completed and the properties are ready to be signed over to the Cohousing project, final calculations must be agreed of the costs of all the construction and development works throughout a project's progress from inception to completion.

Realism is crucial

No group will want delays to their completion dates, with the inevitable wider stress and frustrations that brings. Delays in payments to contractors will lead to difficulties with the completion of work stages. It is therefore crucial that the projected schedule and costings are as realistic as possible so that the level of funds being secured will be sufficient to cover the demands of the construction works.

The necessary paperwork to complete the arrangements of loans and any acceptance of grants will need to be completed by the project's solicitor. The funds can then be arranged forrelease directly to the group's nominated account, ready for the on-site phase.

Examples of costs

An example of a business plan that presents the detail and financial make-up of a current Cohousing project is that for Lowfield Green in Yorkshire, which can be accessed at: www.yorspace.org/uploads/ YorSpace_ Business_Plan_Final.pdf

Here are two examples of costed schemes, described in terms of their constituent costs:

Example A: Forgebank

35 leasehold units sold at market price. Completed 2012 (estimated figures)

1. Early incidental expenses: covered by membership fee of £35/year (£700/year)

2. Early predevelopment cost: covered by a combination of membership fees, interest-free loans from individual members (and interest on invested loans) as well as sweat equity for agreed project management tasks (£3,000)

3. Site purchase: covered by 30% deposits on notional unit prices from 15 households (£600,000)

4. Detailed design, planning and finance arrangement costs: covered by a combination of additional 30% deposits and sweat equity for agreed project management tasks (£100,000)

5. Build costs: covered by a combination of a commercial development loan from Triodos Bank at <70% loan to value, additional 30% deposits, early completions by some members, grant funding for district heating scheme and sweat equity for agreed project management tasks (£8 million)

6. Completion: covered by market value sales less agreed sweat equity

Example B: Halton Senior Cohousing project

14 leasehold market-value units, 4 'discounted' market-value units and 2 'affordable' rented units. At pre-development-stage in 2020.

1. Early Incidental expenses: Covered by membership fee of £25/year (£300/year)

2. Early predevelopment cost: Covered by a combination of membership fees, architects working 'at risk' work and small community-led housing grant from local authority for consultant's advice and feasibility study (£15,000)

3. Detailed design, planning and finance arrangement costs: Covered by Community Led Housing Grant from local authority (£150,000)

4. Site purchase: to be covered by a combination of minimum 20% deposits on for sale units, loans from individual members and <60% development loan from the Ecology Building Society (£450,000)

5. Build costs: to be covered by a combination of a commercial development loan from Ecology Building Society at <80% loan to value, additional deposits, and early completions by some members (£3 million)

6. Completion: to be covered by market value sales, discounted market value sales and mortgage on rented units

Live: Occupation costs and expenses

Finalising sales and rents

A process will need to be agreed for determining the finance required to take up occupation of the dwellings, either as forms of individual household tenures for sale or rent, or as a Mutual Home Ownership scheme.

Market valuations of the completed properties are a standard means of assessing property and scheme values as the basis for agreeing prices for ownership tenures. (Lenders may require assessments of the value of all the properties to reassure them of the worth of the overall scheme to which they are providing their finance, regardless of the period of their loan.)

Leases or ownership agreements for individual properties may include conditions about the prices that can be set for the sale or rent of the property to new members (perhaps in relation to previous prices plus an agreed rate for inflation). The agreements might also stipulate that potential vendors must give the remaining Cohousing members a specified period of time to identify a new household wishing to make the purchase and join the community before the property is listed on the open market (this could be when a form of waiting list becomes useful).

In Mutual Home Ownership schemes, an agreed process established by the scheme will govern the terms on which initial and subsequent amounts of 'equity' could be obtained by individual households, and the basis on which payments will be required, alongside other regular property and service charges. The LILAC scheme has combined the MHO tenure with an obligation for households to meet the community's routine expenses by payments relating to their individual levels of household income.

Rental (or shared ownership) costs for 'affordable' units will need to be set in accordance with national guidelines and local policy for such rents and against a prescribed relationship to market rent levels. Where an external partner like a housing association has been part of the development, that body may provide a Cohousing organisation with a payment for the development and construction costs apportioned to the affordable units (to be used to redeem a portion of the overall loan finance). The association will then gradually recoup that payment from future rental revenue

Undertaking repairs

National legislation – such as The Landlord and Tenant Act 1985 (as amended by the Commonhold and Leasehold Reform Act 2002) in England and Wales sets out the process that landlords are required to go through to be able to pass on the costs of repair works or 'long term agreements' to leaseholders. Cohousing organisations will need to remain familiar with the practical and legislative requirements for how repairs are costed and arranged, either by virtue of being the freeholder of properties that the Cohousing households hold on lease or rent, or by virtue of the households leasing from another organisation.

In a Cohousing community it's normally the case that the decision to go ahead with costly work that will paid collectively has been thoroughly discussed and agreed by the members, but it's worth being aware that if all else fails the members (those who are leaseholder, that is) have these legal rights available to them.

More information can be found at this website: www.lease-advice.org

Advice to groups

What will it finally cost? Will it all be affordable?

Many groups have chosen to produce generic layouts of the dwellings in order to standardise unit costs for the proposed homes. This can also assist later agreements on how properties are ultimately valued according to their size and character.

Larger properties will naturally carry higher costs than smaller ones. However, groups will need to explicitly agree the basis for any final difference in prices or rent levels between them.

The local authority's position on what level of tenure costs will be considered 'affordable' in the future should be discussed with each authority.

When do we have to pay?

It is vitally important that, at the point when construction works have been completed and the property is formally handed over to the Cohousing project that members have their own finances in place to pay what is required to move in.

Who pays for the Common House?

The short answer is that the project does. In the same way as it pays for the landscaping, the access road and paths, the drainage system, the bin store... The Common House is just another part of the infrastructure of a Cohousing project.

Without the construction infrastructure that serves a whole housing scheme, none of the individual houses would be viable to inhabit; without a Common House, the project would not be a viable Cohousing project.

A conventional property developer would routinely add up all the shared infrastructure costs needed for a project and the overall build cost of all the dwellings (adding on a percentage for profit), and then work out the project income from its different components to see whether the scheme was going to be economically viable.

> **The hardest thing we had to do while developing the project was walking the line between being a community group and being a property developer – and knowing when to act like one and not the other**
> *[Established community]*

This holistic overview for the financing of a Cohousing project and its facilities is far more appropriate than looking at it on a 'who-paid-how-much towards-what' basis. This is particularly true for a mixed-tenure Cohousing scheme that could include 'affordable' housing, where some public funds may be used towards meeting the overall project costs including the Common House costs. The common and shared domestic facilities are a crucial element of the social value that Cohousing delivers – over and above a conventional housing scheme – and all residents will benefit from them.

KEY MESSAGE
Project and construction costs need to be considered as a unified whole and funded by contributions from all the dwellings pro rata in relation to their sizes

Live: Property and service charges

Costs of maintaining a project's facilities will be covered by an annually assessed charge agreed by the Cohousing members. This charge can be a flat rate per member or calculated based on the size of individual units, or sometimes both.

As with dealing with the scheme's final construction costs, there is no abstract distinction to make between which tenures will pay ongoing charges, regardless of whether the household's income is from private resources, pensions, or state benefits. How schemes understand the categorisation of expenses as 'charges', however, and what differently labelled 'charges' are supposed to be for, does need to be carefully considered, especially where a Cohousing project has properties under both ownership tenures and rental ones.

Setting rents and service charges will need to be carefully considered and may be something that a project would wish to discuss directly with the local authority at an early stage. Where projects receive public grants towards affordable housing there will be an obligation to use statutory frameworks for annual rent-setting levels.

The ongoing expenses of a Cohousing project might include any or all of the items below:

- building repairs and maintenance;

- service and maintenance contracts;

- 'sinking fund' contributions (set aside to cover expenses of major repairs and replacements);

- small tools and equipment;

- kitchen equipment;

- furnishing renewals;

- utilities and heating in the Common House;

- consumables;

- cleaning fees and materials;

- servicing and maintenance equipment;

- garden tools and equipment;

- tree maintenance;

- children's play equipment;

- waste management;

- area insurance (public liability, common facilities);

- legal fees for the Cohousing body;

- accountancy fees and tax advice;

- bank charges.

Whilst a Cohousing project will want to secure payments from all of its member households, what is included in 'service charges' is likely to differ between leaseholders and affordable rented properties, not in the actual overall scheme costs but in terms of how these are apportioned. For rented properties, much of the management, planned and routine maintenance and repair costs can legitimately be built in as assumptions within the core rent as rent needs to include all relevant property-related expenses, with service charges covering things that are 'additional' and non-property based; for leaseholders, all costs need to be incorporated into a single and regular charging structure that amalgamates distinct cost components.

Projects should consider what separate costs will legitimately be for property maintenance (and included in the rent applied to any rental units) and which expenses can more appropriately be termed 'service charges' (items like 'consumables', 'furnishing' or 'garden tools' in the above list). It should be made clear in the terms of occupancy (leases, rental agreements, etc.) that all charges will be an obligatory part of the shared Cohousing occupation and membership – nothing is optional. This matter becomes particularly relevant when someone is on a low income or not working and makes a claim for welfare assistance towards their housing costs. Members in dwellings that are occupied under home ownership arrangements and leases are not likely to have access to support from welfare benefits to help them meet property costs generally viewed as part of a household's 'living costs', since such benefits are not usually available to property owners.

Households in rental properties, or in shared ownership schemes where a part of the housing cost is through a 'rental sum', will find that local authorities have different assessment criteria for rents and for service charges. The 'property' element of the cost can legitimately be included in the calculation of rent levels, and in the sums sought from benefit payments. The other expenses are usually collected together as 'service charges'.

Rents and service charges could be considered for payment by welfare benefits, where benefit regulations will permit. However, not all service charges are eligible for housing benefit or other housing welfare support and these regulations make a distinction between 'eligible' and 'non-eligible' items – i.e. between what might or might not be accepted for payment under welfare benefit entitlement.

If the rent and service charges set by the Cohousing scheme are not agreed by the local authority, low income households could be required to meet non-eligible service charge costs with a minimal residual income (i.e. from income benefit that is supposed to cover basic living expenses). This could cause hardship for the household and result in the Cohousing community not receiving sufficient income to cover its property costs.

Some schemes abroad have considered establishing a 'hardship' fund for households experiencing financial difficulties, but how each scheme deals with non-payments of charges (and the reasons for this) will be for each scheme to decide. The CLH-Hubs have some details of what legal actions could be applicable here.

Springhill

Use of communal facilities

Charges for such things as communal meals, use of guest rooms and the laundry are usually paid for by the households making use of that facility.

Postscript on financial matters

Some additional Q&A's

Are there different values of the land to calculate within Cohousing sites?

A Cohousing scheme will need to assume that the development as a whole will contribute the resources that will pay for acquiring the site - the price will be for a site that provides for the scheme as a whole and for the total of all of its final elements. The use of the land for the Common House and parking areas and paths and other shared facilities is included in the whole price of the site and is neither paid for nor assessed separately for what will be contributed by the combined total of payments from all of the dwellings. [It is a false notion to consider the footprint of the Common House as 'developable space', since the provision of the facility is integral to the design approach taken to the whole site and uses land in a different manner to mainstream conventional layouts providing roads and hard surfaces to each property.]

The contributions of payments that will be used to cover the site acquisition costs will come from the respective contributions derived from each of the dwellings. An initial financial appraisal will give a first view on how many dwellings the site could contain and how they might generate the contributions to meet the cost of site acquisition.

How are the build costs of a Cohousing scheme finally calculated?

The build costs for a Cohousing scheme will need to be calculated as a unified whole - i.e., that there is no useful purpose in making a distinction between building different elements of the scheme on the chosen site, such as between residential buildings or other shared facilities. The figure for the basic total construction costs is what must be met by the total of whatever resources are being brought into the scheme on its completion (from sales receipts, or grant, or a future rental stream, or whatever) – all of this will need to pay for the costs of the entire construction sum.

What must the Cohousing group do to generate a sufficient cash flow?

The ongoing contribution of finance from a likely combined set of sources (from Cohousing members, from grant, from loans, etc) will all require some initial calculation or consideration in terms of meeting the scheme's overall expenses when they each will need to be met. This will particularly mean be clear about on planning for a suitable flow of cash when it is required. There will not be anything unusual in terms of different sources of finance each contributing towards the total expenses, only that there could be differences in the timescales of when amounts of percentages of some of those contributions may be required at different development and build stages of the project, to help the scheme meet the development costs being incurred at each stage. A scheme may require a 'short-term' development loan to help meet the bulk of its construction costs during the on-site works, or towards site purchase, however agreements can also be set between members of a scheme for how to contribute sums at certain stages - including from a Registered Provider if one is to be involved in the final tenure of some properties.

Should VAT be paid on the provision of a 'Common House'?

The Common Houses that have been built to date in UK Cohousing schemes have been a key part of their overall Cohousing projects from their inceptions - all have been planned for construction as part of the construction stages along with the other residential units (as at ChaCo in Leeds, or LILAC, or Lancaster, etc). Looking at the Government guidance, such as (https://www.gov.uk/guidance/buildings-and-construction-vat-notice-708) buildings that will be created to provide shared dining facilities and other activities that are 'incidental to the enjoyment of the associated residential units' appear to be free of requirements for VAT payment, if they are constructed as part of a combined scheme along with the residential dwellings. There are a number of clauses and paragraphs that provide justification for that basic position – see the text.

What the guidance also seems to state, however, is that the rules were amended a few years ago such that additional facilities created at a later date will require VAT payments. What could be a deciding factor in this is what was included in any original planning approval – was the intention to create the Common House part of the original approval, in which case it could be claimed to be part of an extended or phased programme of construction works, or has it been subject to a separate and later element of intentions or planning approval (even under current 'permitted development' rules…) that shows it to be an afterthought to the original plans. Information from an industry source like 'Buildstore' (https://www.buildstore.co.uk/support-and-inspiration/project-advice/vat-reclaim), can be very helpful useful to look at the basic position about VAT payments and the opportunity to reclaim VAT on new build residential schemes and conversions, etc (although somewhere down the line groups may wish to use the brains of a decent VAT consultant used to dealing with construction projects).

East Whins

Are there different service charges for Cohousing members with different household tenures?

Once a Cohousing scheme is occupied, there will be costs going forward for the basic maintenance and future repair of buildings and facilities, and to cover other 'operating costs' that may arise from agreements between the Cohousing members for how certain equipment of facilities are used in daily life.

a. For properties occupied under one of other form of 'ownership' tenure (full leasehold, or shared ownership, or share equity, or such-like) there is usually a defined separation of responsibility for the maintenance of that property, split between what the household must repair and maintain and what the Cohousing body must maintain, if such a body is the 'freeholder' of the site and ultimately of its buildings. There will then be a separate charge (customarily called a 'service charge') for how the 'ownership' households also pay towards the use and upkeep of the shared facilities. This may be separated between a sum towards the maintenance and repair of the buildings used for shared facilities and a sum for the use of any particular equipment or items inside those facilities, such as equipment for cooking or gardening purposes.

b. There is a parallel set of payments within or attached to the rental payments made by households renting a dwelling, in that the rental sum will itself include a figure for the future upkeep and repair and maintenance of the rented property, and a 'service charge' towards the upkeep of the properties used for shared facilities (including the upkeep of the 'Common House'. Renters should be able to claim Local Housing Allowance ('housing benefit') towards the costs of the rent and this element of the 'service charge' – according to how their own personal circumstances are assessed – but such benefit cannot be claimed for the costs that will relate to a sum for any specifically personal use of equipment (such as a contribution to a 'common kitty' for incidental shared expenses).

c. Some shared-ownership tenancies may have a small cross-over between (a) and (b), given that a portion of their occupancy may require a 'rental' payment on the unbought equity that remains with another owner (such as a housing association, or the Cohousing body as freeholder), and the responsibility between freeholder and occupant-household can vary under such shared arrangements.

On the Brink

Is there any 'tax liability' on a Cohousing body selling leases to its members?

For a company limited by guarantee, which is developing accommodation that will be bought by members at basic cost, there should be no tax liability for the company, and only stamp tax liability for the individual purchasers. If there is some surplus on the unit sales (for example a difference between a unit's development costs - pro rata from the whole scheme – and it's notional 'property value'), the advice to a Cohousing scheme such as Lancaster has been, providing that any of this surplus held and remaining in the company's accounts is used for the mutual benefit and services provided to the company's members, then this would not be taxable. The nature of upholding that 'mutuality' would seem to be the principal point to put across to any advisors to whom groups might turn for assistance.

Trelay, Cornwall

Resources

Build

Live

Design

Finance

The challenge to Cohousing...

The following points present a picture of the environment in which Cohousing exists in the UK.

Strengths

- Award-winning examples of neighbourhood developments
- Schemes appeal to households with private assets and without
- A national body to advise on Cohousing matters and on the development, delivery and finances of Cohousing projects
- Skilled personnel at community-level able to support a range of Cohousing projects
- Core linkages into CLH sector networks

Opportunities

- Growing interest in the delivery of Cohousing from diverse local communities
- Growing interest from older clientele keen to downsize
- Engagement with accredited practitioners from CLH-Hubs
- Ability of Cohousing schemes to cross-fund mixed-tenure dwellings
- Focus on the quality of UK neighbourhoods is very topical
- The new trust in the CLH sector can expand awareness of 'good practice'

Weaknesses

- Being damned by poor comparisons
- A perceived ambiguity about Cohousing's unique characteristics
- Limited engagement from 'finished' schemes
- Uncertainties on ways to fund the communal/shared facilities
- The available Cohousing-specific guidance has not been widely used
- Slowness to identify sufficient professional expertise that understands Cohousing's 'technicalities'
- Limited objective analyses of Cohousing's specific 'added value'
- Few recognised 'Cohousing champions' that new groups could approach

Threats

- Deviant 'models' seizing the Cohousing impetus
- Dismissal of Cohousing site requirements as too demanding
- Perception of Cohousing being elitist and expensive
- Design-led promotion of Cohousing-like layouts, but limited understanding of Cohousing dynamics
- Professional focus on Cohousing-like sociability, but limited control of outcomes by residents
- Reputational risk from imitation Cohousing schemes or services
- Perceptions that the use of private resources is antithetical to the CLH sector

 KEY MESSAGE
Cohousing is a neighbourhood initiative that is a challenge to conventional housing development

and to Cohousing Groups

Potential strengths

- Driven by motivated households to meet their own housing needs
- Can include households with their own assets and without
- Able to utilise professional experience of group members
- Flexibility to create Cohousing projects in new properties or from existing ones
- A recognised 'CLH model' that can utilise support from CLH-Hubs
- Well-established national advice and support networks

Potential opportunities

- Growing interest in delivery of Cohousing across local communities
- Growing interest from stakeholders to support older clientele
- Growing awareness of how to create mixed-tenure schemes
- Focus on the quality of Cohousing neighbourhoods is very topical
- Ample scope to promote the 'social value' of Cohousing outcomes
- Mixed-tenure projects will support local planning policy demands for new and affordable tenures

Potential weaknesses

- Lack of precision from Cohousing group's members on core aims and fundamental demands
- Insufficient engagement with available guidance and advice
- Uncertainty on sources of future funding and discerning payments for joint costs
- Lack of familiarity with engaging professional agents to deliver required services
- Lack of familiarity in negotiations with local planners

Potential threats

- Cohousing 'look-a-likes' can hinder a group's portrayal of Cohousing uniqueness
- A dismissal of Cohousing site requirements as being too demanding
- A continued perception that a Cohousing scheme is 'self-selecting' and elitist
- Dominance by external professionals rather than Cohousing residents
- Ideas that Cohousing projects do not 'fit' with the wider community at large
- No site or building can be acquired to suit the group's vision

 KEY MESSAGE

This guide takes a neutral position on the subject of what tenures a Cohousing project should provide when its homes are to be occupied, however it recommends that a Cohousing group's ambitions should consider the local context in which it seeks to build. Support for the project from external stakeholders is much more likely to happen if a group is willing to provide a mix of residential tenures that will be compliant with the local planning authority's housing and development policies.

Schemes to compare with Cohousing

The SWOT context

UK interest in Cohousing includes various ideas about what the term denotes – perhaps more so than for many of the other models of collaborative and joint housing in the CLH sector. Cohousing clearly inspires people to create shared lifestyles from a host of starting positions, even if some outcomes do not immediately fit the 'core' characteristics in this guide.

The SWOT analysis of Cohousing notes how Cohousing is a real challenge to many established interests and typical ways of working in the UK's housing sector, but it also notes how some interests could claim that Cohousing is already something they provide, and that they have no real need to change.

The core characteristics of Cohousing in this Guide are given as a practical means to remove pressure put on a group's Cohousing ambitions to coerce them into accepting something less – to accept shared dwellings instead of self-contained ones; to accept a common garden or shared laundry room, instead of a proper Common House; to accept the final designs of a professional development team, instead of the Cohousers' vision.

For the numbers of Cohousing projects to increase, it is important that there is no blurring of understanding about what Cohousing groups want, and no manipulative attempt to get Cohousing defined as something it is not.

This need not, however, ignore a real interest in other forms of shared and supportive lifestyles.

Small schemes

Housing provision with shared facilities is clearly desirable to communally-minded groups of households, but not all are big enough to establish the social and financial dynamic of a Cohousing neighbourhood.

For Cohousing-inspired sites on less than half an acre – perhaps with space for only four to eight properties – dwellings could be positioned so that the space(s) between them form a shared area in which different collective or communal activities could take place. It is often possible to enclose that external area (or have a cover over some of it), thereby extending the range of activities it could host. This is the kind of approach taken by Copper Lane in London and in the thinking of Hope Cohousing – the 'Senior' housing project in the Orkneys.

Shared settings for younger households (particularly in some urban centres) could create a definite Cohousing vibe, but in settings which are either too small or too large for the relationship-building that Cohousing is so well-known for. Such modern ideas for shared accommodation often sound like versions of housing co-operatives that have been around for years.

Large sites

Planning and development proposals exist across the UK for thousands of dwellings – including proposals for new 'garden towns' and 'garden villages' and other plans to expand existing residential areas in 'urban extensions'.

Ideas for inter-weaving 'community-led housing' projects into such broader development areas could clearly include Cohousing projects. A tested approach in mainland Europe has been to promote more than one Cohousing scheme in new developments. Clusters of Cohousing dwellings and their common facilities can be found interwoven between other clusters of more conventional dwellings.

But not all sizes of site will be equally suitable for creating a single Cohousing project. This Guide has noted the 'optimum' size of 20 to 50 adults. Even if a potential large site is available (two or more acres), it will be appropriate to consider this for more than one Cohousing scheme.

Using a large site for two Cohousing schemes may seem counterintuitive, and objections could be made that by building two sets of dwellings and common facilities the group would miss out on economies of scale that could be gained from building just one larger scheme, but a larger scale project would lead to less opportunity to develop the community relationships so important to Cohousing. (One larger set of community facilities may in fact not result in much cost reduction.)

'Co-living' schemes

Ideas about 'co-living' are in vogue – they provide opportunities for a shared living environment and respond to modern desires for an accessible and convivial location close to city centres.

"Co-living can be broadly defined as an alternative housing model which seeks to promote social contact through the living environment" (University of Cambridge report on supporting vulnerable older people).

This would seem to share attributes with Cohousing, but there are key differences in the way such an 'option' is being promoted by the development industry.

> *For today's working professional, co-living is often about much more than simply sharing a property; it's a personal choice and a way of life. For some it's about meeting new people having recently moved to a new city for work. For others it's a great way of establishing new friendships and building a brand new social life.*
>
> *[Mainstream co-living developer]*

Co-living lifestyles could definitely have an appeal, especially to younger people in areas with affordability issues (like London and Brighton), but it is not appropriate to consider extensive numbers of studio-size bedsits, even with private use of gyms and leisure facilities, as synonymous with Cohousing's design, scale or intent.

> *I can see [the] point about getting some clear messages out there about the distinctiveness of Cohousing – this is important, especially for the external mainstream audience.*
>
> *[CLH-Hub]*

Finance Design Live Build

Diversity: Challenging Assumptions

I like the idea of diversity, but my local area doesn't seem very diverse

Diversity comes in many forms, not all of which are visible or immediately obvious. Be open and honest: which aspects of diversity is your community actively welcoming? Consider age, sexualities and gender identities, ethnic background, income, education, occupation, beliefs, abilities, lifestyles, and personalities and look for ways to foster diversity within your community.

❝ Diversity helps us to know ourselves better and so it is essential for my personal development. ❞
[Housing Diversity Network]

We've tried recruiting more widely but some groups in society are not interested in Cohousing

Is this fact or assumption? Many people will not be familiar with Cohousing. Are your recruitment efforts reaching those people? Are you growing 'organically' by word of mouth? If so, is your social network diverse? Can you take steps to broaden or change your networks by going beyond current friendship, work, or social groups?

Cohousing as a movement is still in its early phases. Claude Hendrickson of Leeds Community Homes has studied diversity issues in housing and believes people are more likely to be attracted to community-led housing when they see greater diversity in leadership of those groups.

How might others perceive your group? Is there something about your project that comes across as exclusive to other people?

Too much diversity might undermine balance or cohesion in the community

❝ By deliberately developing diversity in the expected closeness of Cohousing, I think I am inviting different perspectives to challenge my outlook and keep me learning. Diversity means surprises, frustration, health, patience, laughter, adjustments, [and an] ongoing re-evaluation [of] priorities. ❞
[Cohousing Enabler]

Some people believe the key to creating successful communities is to recruit people of a 'like mind'. However, groups that set out on this basis often run into problems as many discover the field of things they initially believe they hold in common is more limited than they thought, and an oversimplistic basis for addressing issues of living together.

Cohesion can be used as another word for comfort; if a group feels very comfortable, it could be a sign of stagnation. Some believe that a healthy community should have a slight sense of discomfort and constructive friction as different opinions, positions, ideas, and cultures are expressed and welcomed without progress being hindered.

Communities may also want to consider themselves open and connected to their localities. This may include being open to embracing comment and criticism, which can be welcomed as a means to renewal and growth.

All communities change and develop over time as new people join, others leave, and circumstances change. Common ground between members can be established through agreeing a vision and a set of values, so that new members know what to expect. Groups can then review and assess how much of the common ground and shared goals represents a healthy collective culture. They can review progress to see whether individuals feel able to express views, be heard, and share differences and whether unconscious bias has crept in. Having a healthy community culture gives people confidence that differences can be acknowledged, whilst progress is achieved.

To establish a sustainable, healthy Cohousing community, groups should build solid, transparent practices for decision-making, conflict resolution, membership, shared listening and so forth. These ground rules create a solid base on which to build a diverse, but cohesive community.

> **❝Embracing diversity is time-consuming, especially in decision-making, and is likely to cause (healthy) conflict. But that provides a great arena for creative solutions.❞**
> [UKCN Diversity & Inclusion Sub-group]

> **❝An improved representation of traditionally under-represented groups will present your cohousing community as a champion of improving equality of opportunity to current and prospective residents.❞**
> [Mushtaq Khan, CEO, Housing Diversity Network]

Diversity: Overcoming common barriers

Money, time, skills and values are common perceived barriers to diversity in Cohousing communities, but often the biggest barrier is outlook – the way we think about diversity. This section looks at potential ways of overcoming some of the barriers to diversity.

Money

Arguably, who has money and who doesn't in society is often a matter of good fortune or inheritance. Cohousing groups need to talk about money and their financial plans openly, early, and often, without shame or embarrassment. Being able to take the sting of shame and judgement out of discussions will help Cohousing groups build goodwill and sound judgements. Assumptions and decisions on finance affect choice of location, type of funding build, size of community, and ultimately who can and can't join a community. Decisions about money will also affect whether the community holds together or divides in later generations. At the same time, Cohousing groups need to be realistic about the challenges of competing in the market for land and housing, and compromises and creativity may be needed. Whether a Cohousing scheme is rental or home-ownership-based there are several considerations groups can take to further diversity and inclusion in terms of affordability. Cohousing is increasingly accepted as a design model applicable for capital funding for affordable housing (below market sales or rent). If you are considering this approach, you may want to explore social commitments or legal clauses to avoid property prices escalating in the future when members leave or sell. Some Cohousing groups may subsequently buy up previously-bought units to create more affordable rental homes over

time. Some generous Cohousing members even bequeath properties to communities for this purpose. Mutual home ownership societies (MHOS) provide an alternative to rent/home ownership and allow those with equity to live alongside those without or without significant equity, on an equal basis. MHOS will evolve and simplify over time. For more information about finance options see the 'Potential sources' in the FINANCE section further on in this Guide.

Time

New housing developments typically take between five and seven years to establish. Can everyone wait that long or stay the course? This timescale might favour those planning retirement more than those beginning careers or with young families; expectations need to be realistic. Being community-led, Cohousing can require a great deal of participation by volunteers to attend meetings, committees, social events, and shared meals. It is easy for Cohousing schemes driven by voluntary participation to be led by those with most time to commit rather than equitably. Consideration should be given to community members short on time due to jobs, family commitments, a health condition or other reasons. Consider creative ways to encourage involvement from community members – or potential members – who aren't able to commit as much time as others. For example, many groups use online tools to offer ways for people to read opinions, join discussions and place a vote when they have time rather than when a specific meeting is arranged. Combining face-to-face meetings with online meeting software such as Zoom or Microsoft Teams is increasingly common and can allow people to join when they are at work or away from the area. Setting up a

Cohousing community is a chance to find new ways of doing things. Be creative; talk to other groups; share your experiences.

Skills

Developing housing projects can be hugely demanding and it is easy for those with skills in organising, decision-making or project management, or those most confident in groups to end up having a far greater say than others. For some people, the language used in meetings can be off-putting. Social skills in teams or groups are vital to being part of a community. It is important to consider neuro-diversity and how it might show up in practice. For example, those unable to read social cues or unfamiliar with expected behaviours might not be seen as a good fit. However, group skills and decisions can be agreed and learnt, or meetings can be adapted to include a wider range of communication and focus on what's really agreed as important. Conversely, some people with highly valued skills such as project management or finance might be given a higher position in the hierarchy than others. Pay attention to the culture you are creating when you meet to ensure inclusivity.

Values

If your group feels strongly about aiming for diversity and inclusion, you may want to include this in a formal list of values so that everyone is reminded of its importance to your group.

Outlook

Our personal outlooks are usually developed over many years; changing them can be key to embracing diversity. A good starting point can be to reflect upon the diversity within our own bodies – our strengths, weaknesses, shapes, sizes, and abilities – and to recognise the diversity that is woven into the fabric of life all around us and which enriches our lives when we are open to it.

> *Community members should discuss what they would be willing to give up – attitudinally and/or financially – to include diverse members. The need for personal introspection doesn't end once the houses are constructed and residents unpack their boxes. Over time, the community evolves, and residents need to keep unpacking their personal histories and values as families move, people pass away, and new neighbours arrive.*
> [Alan O'Hashi, Communities Magazine]

> *Intentional communities tend to have strong shared value systems, and I think they would make wonderful environments in which to do this work of transmuting White Fragility into White Humility.*
> [Murphy Robinson, Communities Magazine]

Forgebank Cohousing

Managing communal facilities long term

- Forgebank is a Cohousing community in the village of Halton outside of Lancaster, developed by Lancaster Cohousing.

- Forgebank has been occupied since 2012 and comprises 41 private homes with a shared Common House and shared outdoor space. All homes were built to certified PassivHaus standards and the community predominantly uses renewable energy generated on-site.

- Lancaster Cohousing is a company limited by guarantee. Directors are elected annually for two-year terms and are responsible to the membership (made up of all leaseholders and tenants at Forgebank).

- All decisions are taken by members of Lancaster Cohousing in General Meetings through a consensus decision-making process. All adults living at Forgebank take part in the maintenance and management of the site and community.

- Most homes are leasehold properties in which Lancaster Cohousing retains the freehold; there are also six slightly separate properties which were sold freehold to help finance the development.

- Development was financed through a loan from Triodos Bank and borrowing from members.

The Lancaster Cohousing project at Forgebank is a Cohousing development of 41 two- and three-bed family homes and one-bed flats, which maximises eco-construction techniques and principles. The Common House at the heart of the site includes a large communal kitchen and dining area as well as a children's playroom, laundry facilities and guest bedrooms. There is communal outdoor space and residents use a communal car-pool. Lancaster Cohousing also manages a workspace nearby for small enterprises or freelancers, which is available to Forgebank residents at a reduced rate.

Lancaster Cohousing is registered as a company limited by guarantee with directors elected by members annually for two years at the General Meeting. All leaseholders and tenants are members and any adult living in the community can become a member. Directors report to the monthly General Meeting where decisions are taken by all members through a consensus decision-making process.

Social interaction between Cohousing members is a key value of the scheme. Members can take part in multiple communal meals per week and other planned community activities. As well as the Common House, there is also a covered pedestrianised street and external spaces around the homes where residents can meet and children can play.

Sustainability is the second key value of the scheme and is central to the ethos at Forgebank in both the design and the lifestyle of the Cohousing community. All homes are built to certified PassivHaus standards. Energy is mostly supplied by a 160kW hydroelectric scheme that was developed alongside the Cohousing project by a group from Halton village and from solar panels on the community roofs. The project was designed by the residents with architects Eco Arc and built by local building firm Whittles Construction.

Lancaster Cohousing funded the purchase of the site privately through the founding members. The total development cost was financed by a mix of lending from future residents to

Lancaster Cohousing and a bank loan from Triodos Bank. Members loaned Lancaster Cohousing up to 30% of the cost of their homes pre-development and when homes were completed members paid the rest of the purchase cost of their homes either directly or through a mortgage lender. Most of the homes are leasehold properties (Lancaster Cohousing owns the freehold) with the leases containing stipulations for members which are specific to the responsibilities of living in the Cohousing community. If members wish to sell their homes on, they can do so at market value. Lancaster Cohousing keeps a waiting list of interested parties and the new buyers or tenants must be accepted as members of Lancaster Cohousing before moving in. Six properties on the west side of the site were sold as freehold properties as part of the financing of the whole scheme.

All residents take part in the management and upkeep of the scheme with all adult residents contributing around 10 hours a month including specific cleaning of common areas on a rota system. In addition, every member agrees to contribute to the cooking and washing up of at least one communal meal a month. All households must pay a service charge per member of the household which is set annually at the General Meeting. This covers all the costs of upkeep of the communal areas, insurance and audit fees.

Learning points

- Cohousing communities need to establish clear ways of working and managing shared facilities from the outset.

- A leasehold model allows the Cohousing group to collectively own the communal space and control the use of the private homes whilst still providing the benefits of home ownership to leaseholders and allowing the development to finance itself through the sale of the homes.

- Groups need to plan for the long term with flexibility in their financial planning and their decision-making processes.

- It is possible for Cohousing groups to access loan finance for their development but they will also need significant additional capital input. If schemes are not developing an affordable housing product, this will need to come from secondary lending or member equity. In this case, this additional funding came from member equity.

Forgebank

Build

Live

Finance Design

Lowfield Green Housing Co-op

Cohousing via Mutual Home Ownership

- Lowfield Green Housing Co-operative (LGHC) will deliver York's first environmentally sustainable, mutually owned, Cohousing community.

- Mutual Home Ownership means that the homes are collectively owned by a co-operative society in which all the residents are members.

- Membership of Lowfield Green Housing Co-operative is contingent on residents paying a monthly contribution to the MHO scheme, based on the size of the property and equity purchased.

- 19 homes will be built, including one- and two-bedroom flats and two-, three- and four-bedroom houses, plus a Common House and other shared facilities at the core of the development.

- Finance for the project will be a combination of mortgage finance, grant funding, deposits from residents, and a loan from Yorspace CLT, the body that has promoted and helped to develop the overall scheme.

Lowfield Green Housing Co-operative (LGHC) is a Mutual Home Ownership (MHO) society, which is a fully mutual society that will own the properties its members occupy. This differs from other types of shared ownership wherein an institution retains part ownership of a property. In Mutual Home Ownership there is no outside institution owning any of the properties; they are fully owned by the MHO scheme and the members collectively own the MHO scheme.

The Lowfield Green Cohousing project will create York's first Cohousing neighbourhood on a lease of 0.75 acres of land from York's first community land trust (CLT), YorSpace. YorSpace CLT negotiated the purchase of the Lowfield Green site from City of York Council and has agreed a subsequent 999-year lease between YorSpace and Lowfield Green Housing Co-operative.

YorSpace led the pre-development stage of the project, during which time YorSpace members volunteered to join the working teams for the co-operative's development. These members are continuing their work during the development stage and will become residents of LGHC at the post-development stage when the homes are completed and ready for occupation.

Planning permission was granted in March 2019 for 19 homes including one- and two-bedroom flats and two-, three- and four-bedroom houses, giving the community scope to house people at many life stages, from single professionals and retirees to large families, creating a diverse, intergenerational community. The development plans also include communal space and facilities, with a large shared kitchen diner, laundrette, guest accommodation and flexible office space. These shared facilities are the core of the Cohousing ethos and create a hub around which a warm and thriving community can grow.

The homes have been designed along One Planet Living principles and the costings have included the use of bio-based sustainable construction materials, such as hemp, straw and wood fibre, that will create high performance homes that are healthy and comfortable to live in and extremely economical to run. On-site power generation using photovoltaics has been included in the scheme design, plus extensive bicycle storage and only 12 car parking spaces for the 19 homes, meaning a low carbon lifestyle will be built into the fabric of life at Lowfield Green.

The project has been conceived specifically to create homes that are affordable now and in perpetuity. The co-operative will achieve this by working with YorSpace CLT, which has undertaken the pre-development work for the site. It will supply the homes to the residents at cost. Construction will be funded through a mixture of mortgage finance, grant funding, residents' deposits and a loan from YorSpace CLT. The total cost of construction has been modelled to ensure residents' monthly contributions are 80% of similar market rates and will allow the co-operative to repay its mortgage obligations (interest and capital), meet regular running costs, create a reserve for planned maintenance and repay the loan to YorSpace CLT. As the capital of the mortgage and the loan from YorSpace are paid off, residents will accrue equity in Lowfield Green Housing Co-operative. In this way, the residents own a releasable share of the co-operative. Upon leaving the co-operative, residents are able to take their equity with them and the co-operative sells the equity to the next resident. This innovative mechanism combines the strength of co-operative ownership whilst protecting the LGHC from demutualisation.

Learning points

● Cohousing neighbourhoods can be established via developers that have chosen to use Mutual Home Ownership models as the basis for economic and household inclusion.

● YorSpace creates Mutual Home Ownership societies to achieve its vision of combining social and ethical share investment funding with co-operative ownership for residents.

● There is a legal development services agreement in place between Lowfield Green Housing Co-operative and YorSpace CLT.

● YorSpace will provide advice and act as an employer's agent and clerk of works for the Lowfield Green Housing Co-operative. As the clerk of works, YorSpace will ensure that the buildings are delivered as stipulated in the contract signed with the building professionals.

Marmalade Lane Cohousing

A project initiated by a local authority

- Marmalade Lane is a Cohousing development in Cambridgeshire, developed through an initiative by Cambridge City Council in response to years of effort and commitment by Cambridge Cohousing Group.

- Cambridge Cohousing Limited is a company limited by guarantee. Every property owner is required to be a company member. Every household can have one person as a director, and decision-making is based on consensus.

- Marmalade Lane was completed in 2019 and comprises 42 private homes with a shared Common House and shared outdoor space. The homes are a mix of leasehold one- and two-bedroom apartments and freehold three-, four- and five-bedroom houses.

- A competitive tendering process provided good land value for Cambridge City Council.

- Project development was financed by the developer and used modern methods of construction (MMC), which perform to high environmental standards.

- Marmalade Lane won a 2019 RIBA National Award, the Richard Fielden Award, at the 2019 Housing Design Awards, and was the overall winner at the 2020 RTPI Awards for Planning Excellence.

Marmalade Lane Cohousing in Cambridgeshire is a development of 42 private homes with a shared Common House and shared outside space, completed in 2019. The homes are a mix of one- and two-bed apartments and three-, four- and five-bed houses. The Common House includes a large kitchen, lounge, laundry facilities, children's playroom and flexible spaces for meetings and classes. It also includes guest bedrooms and a workshop. At the centre of the development is a large, shared, south-facing garden with areas for relaxation, play and food-growing.

The project came about through an innovative partnership between Cambridge City Council (the landowner), Cambridge Cohousing Group (future residents) and private developers. After the financial crash in 2007, the landowners, Cambridge City Council, decided to designate the site for a Cohousing development to maximise a capital receipt and to create sustainable housing with high environmental performance.

A new Cohousing group focussed on this site, formed from the original group that had been working since 2000 to persuade the city council to support Cohousing ideas. A new legal entity was established – Cambridge Cohousing Limited – as a company limited by guarantee with a large board of potentially 42 directors. The board is supported by working groups (finance, process, outreach, maintenance, Common House, grounds, transport, food, community, tech, gym and workshop). Proposals are developed through dialogue and active agreement is sought. The ability to move to majority voting if consensus cannot be achieved has been retained.

Cambridge Cohousing Limited drew up a client brief for an intergenerational community with a wide range of sizes and price points. Once outline planning permission had been obtained, a competitive tender took place and TOWN and Trivselhus were appointed in July 2015 as the 'enabling' developers. The design phase was organised into workstreams, enabling the Cohousing group to be involved with the professional team as the design was developed after the successful bid. Members were offered options to customise their homes and they worked with the professional team to codesign the shared spaces. Full planning approval for 42 properties and the Common House was obtained in 2016.

The homes are built close to PassivHaus standard, with air source heat pumps and mechanical ventilation and heat recovery (MVHR) systems. The Common House and apartments used prefabricated cross-laminated timber panels from Sweden.

The enabled development model made the process relatively straightforward for the Cohousing group members, with a low financial cost or risk to members. At completion, 30 of the 42 properties had been purchased by members as a result of the Cohousing group's own marketing activity.

The properties were sold at open market value with discounts for early commitment and prices were 'fixed' before completion date. Cambridge Cohousing maintains a waiting list of prospective future residents, and when a resident wishes to sell a property, they are required to give Cambridge Cohousing eight weeks to offer it to the waiting list at full market value before it may be sold on the open market.

Learning points

● A community can be recruited and built around the opportunity offered by a site, as is common in 'building group' projects in continental Europe.

● Local authorities can be key to unblocking the challenges Cohousing groups face in finding sites.

● The 'enabled' development model made the process relatively straightforward for the Cohousing group members, with a low financial cost/risk to themselves, and led to a good proportion of committed purchasers being involved from the outset.

● It is important to develop a clear design brief but be ready to stay flexible and pragmatic whilst letting the developer's professional team do the detailed work.

● Make sure purchasers understand the practical implications of an off-plan purchase. The two-stage procurement process focused on quality before introducing price and was highly effective for a project which was innovative in its design.

Cannock Mill Cohousing

A Senior Cohousing project

- Cannock Mill Cohousing is a mix of self-contained properties built around the renovation of a derelict mill on a challenging site in Colchester

- The scheme comprises 23 new-build private homes, with a shared Common House and facilities in the mill building.

- All homes were built to certified 'PassivHaus' standards and to Lifetime Homes standards.

- Cannock Mill Cohousing is a company limited by guarantee.

- Development was financed through assets and borrowing from the Cohousing members, assisted with a loan facility from Homes England.

Cannock Mill Cohousing Colchester is a community developed upon the following values:

- good neighbourliness – in supporting each other within the Cohousing community and in making a positive contribution to the social, economic and cultural life of the locality, Old Heath, Colchester and the surrounding area;

- active ageing – as a way of encouraging participation, health, independence and environmental awareness;

- eco-awareness – embodied in low energy design, sharing of resources and

The age range of the group is currently from the late fifties onwards, with the majority in their sixties, however membership is not restricted to any age range, gender, sexual orientation, religious or ideological or political belief, or postcode.

The new development is a mix of one- and two-bedroom flats and 17 two- and three-bedroom houses (some with garages) designed by Anne Thorne Architects and built by Jerram Falkus Construction Ltd. The physical focus of the site is the Common House that has been sited within the pre-existing mill building. The renovation of Cannock Mill itself (dating from

1611), has provided a range of spaces including a professionally planned kitchen, opening into a flexible dining room/meeting room, a sitting room/library, guest bedrooms and workshops.

The new buildings are designed to achieve the externally recognised PassivHaus standard: all houses have living green roofs; the homes are built in timber frame cassettes with recycled newspaper insulation; flooring is renewable bamboo; and bespoke kitchens avoid MDF. Externally, the finish is 'self-coloured' lime render, in different natural mineral colours, so it should not require repainting.

There are extensive external communal gardens and restoration of the mill pond is being planned (including checking its suitability for 'wild swimming'!)

Members have agreed to minimise car use, in line with the community's 'eco' aspirations and a car-pooling scheme encourages people to dispense with private cars.

A loan facility agreed with Homes England (HE) was significant in managing the cashflow for the staged payments for the construction works. Several directors were also able to make interest-free loans to the company and reduce further drawdown of the Homes England loan. All homes are leasehold properties, with Cannock Mill Cohousing owning the freehold.

The overall membership includes households with significant professional and managerial experience, and this proved invaluable to the self-management of the different phases of the overall scheme development. Since the project began, all members have belonged to at least two subgroups, working on different areas such as building, finance, communications, membership and social activities.

For further information: www.cannockmillcohousingcolchester.co.uk

Learning points

- During recladding work on the mill, rot was identified in some structural timbers. A remedial proposal had to be designed and agreed with the local authority before repairs could take place as the Mill is a listed building.

- Extensive professional and managerial experience within the group's membership meant that there were substantial skills available to deal with site development tasks.

Examples of Cohousing tenures

Tenures within the projects of current UK Cohousing Network members

Social rents

Bridport Cohousing
Threshold Centre

Affordable rents

Threshold Centre
New Ground
Lancaster Senior Cohousing
ChaCo Chapeltown

Mutual Home Ownership

Trelay Community
LILAC
Lowfield Green

Shared ownership

Bridport Cohousing
Threshold Centre
On the Brink
Lancaster Senior Cohousing
ChaCo Chapeltown

Leasehold ownership

Springhill
Cannock Mill
New Ground
Laughton Lodge
Marmalade Lane
Forgebank
Threshold Centre
Lancaster Senior Cohousing

Outright sale

Copper Lane

Note: Some projects have more than one tenure
(no UKCN members use shared equity tenures at present)

Resources

Books about Cohousing

- **The Cohousing Handbook: Building a Place for Community** *Hanson* New Society Publications 2004 ISBN 0865715173

- **Thinking About Cohousing** *Martin Field* Diggers and Dreamers Publications 2004 ISBN 0951494570

- **Reinventing Community: Stories from the Neighborhoods of Cohousing** *David Wann* Fulcrum Group 2005 ISBN 1555915019

- **Sustainable Community: Learning from the Cohousing Model** *G Meltzer* Trafford 2005 ISBN 1412049946

- **The Senior Cohousing Handbook** *Charles Durrett* New Society Publications 2009 ISBN 0865716110

- **Living Together – Cohousing Ideas and Realities Around the World** *Dick Urban* Vestro 2010 ISBN 9174157388

- **Creating Cohousing** *McCamant and Durrett* New Society Publications 2011 ISBN 0865716722

- **Cohousing in Britain** Diggers and Dreamers Publications 2011 ISBN 0951494570

- **Cohousing in Britain (Vol 2)** Diggers and Dreamers Publications 2023

- **Creating Community-Led and Self-Build Homes** *Martin Field* 2020 ISBN 9781447344391

- **Senior Cohousing Primer** *Durrett and Nilsson* Habitat Press 2017 ISBN-10: 0945929048

- **Senior Cohousing: A New Way Forward for Active Older Adults** *Sherry Cummings* Springer 2019 ISBN 3030253619

- **Contemporary Cohousing in Europe: Towards Sustainable Cities?** Kindle edition 2019 ASIN: B07WGQBTW2

- **CoHousing Inclusive: Self-organised, community-led housing for all** *Jovis Verlag* Bilingual edition 2019 ISBN 9783868594621

Books about community dynamics

- **The Collective Housing Handbook** *Sarah Eno and Dave Treanor* Laurieston Hall Publications 1982 ISBN 0950831514

- **Building United Judgment** Fellowship for Intentional Community 1999 ISBN 0960271465

- **Creating a Life Together** *Diana Leafe Christian* New Society Publications 2003 ISBN 0865714711

- **Head, Heart and Hands: Lessons in Community Building** *Shari Leach* Johnson Printing 2005 ASIN: B003FCUW6W

- **Finding Community** *Diana Leafe Christian* New Society Publications 2007 ISBN 0865715785

- **Come Hell or High Water: A Handbook on Collective Process Gone Awry** *Vannucci and Singer* AK Press 2010 ISBN 1849350183

- **Let's Talk About Money: A Conversation Guide for Intentional Communities** *E Weaver* Create Space 2001 ISBN 1478148640

- **Facilitation at a Glance! Your Pocket Guide to Facilitation** *Ingrid Bens* Goal/QPC 2012 ISBN 1576811379

- **A Consensus Handbook: Co-operative decision-making for activists, co-ops and communities** Seeds for Change 2013 ISBN 0957587104

- **Wisdom of Communities** Vol 1-4 Fellowship for Intentional Community 2018 ISBN 0999588583

Books and articles about cohousing design

- **Cohousing** *K McCamant and C Durrett* (1994) 2011 ISBN 0898155398

- **Creating Cohousing** *K McCamant and C Durrett* (2011) ISBN 9780865716728

- **Community Enhanced Design – Cohousing and other high-functioning neighbourhoods** *Charles Durrett* (2022) www.cohousingco.com

- **The Cohousing Approach to Lifetime Neighbourhoods** *M Brenton* (2008) www.housingcare.org/downloads/kbase/3140.pdf

- **Senior Cohousing** *M Brenton* (2013) ISBN 9781859359266

- **The Senior Cohousing Handbook** *Charles Durrett* (2009) ISBN 0865716110

- **Cohousing in Britain – a Diggers & Dreamers Review** (2011) ISBN 9780954575731

- **Thinking About Cohousing** *Martin Field* (2004) ISBN 0951494570

Useful websites – General Information

- **Rural Housing Scotland** www.ruralhousingscotland.org

- **The Cohousing Association of America** www.cohousing.org

- **Canadian Cohousing Network** www.cohousing.ca

- **Diggers and Dreamers: Intentional Community in Britain** www.diggersanddreamers.org.uk

- **Foundation for Intentional Community** www.ic.org

- **Communities Magazine** #178 (Spring 2018) – Class, Race, and Privilege
  www.ic.org/community-bookstore/product/communities-magazine-178-spring-2018-class-race-privilege

- **The Racial Justice Network** (courses unlearning racism, unconscious bias and cultural awareness) www.racialjusticenetwork.co.uk/our-work/unlearning-racism

- **Housing Diversity Network** (equality and inclusion training) www.housingdiversitynetwork.co.uk

- **Ted** (talk on cultural intelligence) youtu.be/izeiRjUMau4

- **Non-violent Communication** www.nvc-uk.com

- **Seeds of Change** (experienced campaigners and co-operators, offering training, facilitation, online resources and other support for campaigns, community groups and co-operatives. Also sell the Consensus Handbook) www.seedsforchange.org.uk

- **Sociocracy for All** (training and support on inclusive, consent-based decision making systems) www.sociocracyforall.org/community

- **Roffey Park Institute** (facilitation skills) www.roffeypark.ac.uk

- **International Coaching Federation** (facilitation skills)
  www.icf-events.org/icw/art-of-effective-facilitation

- **Community Resolve** (mediation skills) www.henwilkinson.info

- **Process Work UK** (working with power dynamics, hierarchies, rank) www.processworkuk.org

- **Communities Housing Trust** (the leading organisation for facilitating community-led housing in Scotland) www.chtrust.co.uk

- **South of Scotland Community Housing** www.sosch.org

● Useful websites – Cohousing Schemes

● **Bridport Cohousing** (English intergenerational social housing units example) www.bridportcohousing.org.uk

● **Cannock Mill** (English senior example) www.cannockmillcohousingcolchester.co.uk

● **Canon Frome** (English retrofit example) www.canonfromecourt.org.uk

● **Chapeltown Cohousing** (English new build and affordable homes in a multicultural and ethnically diverse area example) www.chapeltowncohousing.org.uk

● **Forgebank** (English new build example) www.lancastercohousing.org.uk

● **Dôl-Llys Hall** (Welsh new build example) www.dol-llys.co.uk

● **East Whins** (Scottish new build example) www.4allsentientbeings.wordpress. com/2015/08/08/east-whins-cohousing-cluster-at-findhorn

● **Laughton Lodge** (English retrofit example) www.laughtonlodge.org

● **LILAC** (English new build example) www.lilac.coop

● **New Ground** (English senior, women only affordable example) www.owch.org.uk

● **On the Brink** (English retrofit example) www.onthebrink.community

● **Springhill** (English new build example) www.springhillcohousing.com

● **Sturts Farm** (English social housing for people with learning disabilities example) www.sturtscommunitytrust.org.uk

● **Threshold Centre** (English retrofit example) www.thresholdcentre.org.uk

● **Thundercliffe Grange** (English retrofit example) www.thundercliffegrange.co.uk/history

● **Trelay** (English retrofit example) www.trelay.org

● See also the current list of projects and other Cohousing groups on the UKCN website: www.cohousing.org.uk/members-directory

Lightning Source UK Ltd.
Milton Keynes UK
UKHW020714081222
413492UK00007B/67

9 781838 472528